RETURN *to*
TITANIC

RETURN *to*
TITANIC

A NEW LOOK AT THE
WORLD'S MOST FAMOUS LOST SHIP

ROBERT D. BALLARD
WITH MICHAEL S. SWEENEY

NATIONAL GEOGRAPHIC

WASHINGTON, D.C.

CONTENTS

PAGE 1: *ROV* Hercules *photographs the base of a collapsed crane on the stern afterdeck.*

PAGE 2-3: *Rusticles, "rust icicles," pushed by currents slant along R.M.S.* Titanic's *bow in 2004.*

PAGE 4: *Stunned survivors of the* Titanic *disaster gather with bedding and blankets.*

TITANIC IS MANY THINGS to many people. To some it embodies the overstuffed opulence of the Edwardian era. Poetic souls find the best and worst of human nature in its final hours. Others view its fate as a cautionary tale about the folly of arrogance.

In the years since I led the team that discovered *Titanic* in 1985, I have watched it play new parts on the world stage. Graveyard. Time capsule. Celluloid star.

Now *Titanic* has assumed its most crucial role. The magnificent ship rests at a crossroads of history, and the choice of its path will affect undersea exploration for decades to come. On one side of the debate are those who argue that the best route to preserve such wrecks is to retrieve any artifacts that have aesthetic, historic, or sentimental value. They send submersibles to the ocean floor and salvage what they find there. On the other side are those who see *Titanic* as a wondrous museum to be appreciated without being violated.

Without apology, I can count myself among the latter.

Titanic, nearly 13,000 feet below the surface of the North Atlantic, isn't going anywhere. Left alone, it will remain a perfect window of life—and death—in 1912. But as deep-sea technology becomes more widespread, the risk to *Titanic* and other precious shipwrecks grows ever greater. Damaged and picked over, *Titanic* is less of a ship now than two decades ago. Witnessing what has happened to the stately queen saddens those who wish to preserve her. When I consider the darkest possible future for *Titanic,* I think of the loss to tomorrow's generations.

My mind then turns to Gettysburg.

My family traveled to Williamsburg, Virginia, from England in 1635. Family members soon went their separate ways. One branch of Ballards stayed in Virginia's plantation country, but the patriarch started a new branch in New England. During the Civil War, the descendants of the Virginia Ballards and the descendants of the New England Ballards met at the Battle of Gettysburg in 1863. Both branches counted their own among the 51,000 who died during the bloodiest battle ever fought in the Western Hemisphere. Perhaps Ballards, Northern and Southern, literally killed one another.

The grounds of Gettysburg National Military Park are well-preserved, thanks to an 1895 act of Congress that established it as a memorial. I have walked the land, contemplating the sacrifices made by my ancestors. Next to a clump of birch trees I came upon a sign marking the farthest advance of Pickett's Charge, which sent 12,000 Confederate troops into the withering fire of Union lines and began the South's long fall.

When I saw that sign, I cried. The realization that I stood where history turned, where thousands died in acts of courage, honor, and devotion, opened the gates of emotion. I was there on the very spot, as my ancestors had been in their final moments, and I was transformed by the experience.

So it was with *Titanic*. I had not planned to cry when I visited it either, but I did. A sense of the continuity of history overwhelmed me.

In 1986, one year after watching *Titanic* magically appear in the video monitors of the research vessel *Knorr*, I returned with a science team and explored the wreckage in *Alvin*, a three-man submersible.

At the end of our eighth dive, we left a memorial plaque on the stern, where so many of the ship's passengers died. As we ascended, I focused a camera on the plaque. Higher and higher we rose, and yet the image of the plaque stayed centered in the video screen. The polished metal gleamed against the darkened, rusty, silt-covered poop deck. I realized then that tears were pouring from my eyes.

To witness the *Titanic* in those silent depths, to feel so close to tragedy, was just like visiting Gettysburg. Each scene represented a dark moment in history. Each still speaks to us over the gulf of

TEN DAYS *after a photographer snapped this postcard image of R.M.S.* Titanic *at the Southampton dock, its bow was driven nearly anchor-deep into the muddy ocean bottom.*

years. The loss of *Titanic* resonates with our modern world whenever we feel a loss of innocence. The death of John F. Kennedy. The shocking destruction of the space shuttles *Challenger* and *Columbia.* The terrorist attacks of September 11, 2001. Such events shake our optimism, our confidence, and our belief that human beings control their destiny. Yet we would not want a world without *Titanic* or Gettysburg. Saving them, and all their rich meaning, guarantees that voices of history will speak to our grandchildren.

Ensuring *Titanic*'s preservation was at the heart of the expedition I undertook in the summer of 2004. I wanted to document the damage of the last 18 years, demonstrate a better way to appreciate *Titanic,* and beat the drum of public opinion to give the ship the same kind of protection that has shielded other national and international treasures. I wanted to make *Titanic* a test case for dealing with the thousands of shipwrecks still lying unexplored in international waters.

That was a tall order, but one I relished. The mission of a lifetime began with a return to *Titanic.*

CHAPTER ONE
FINDING *the* TITANIC

R.M.S. TITANIC *at sea on its first and only voyage.*
Three funnels emitted smoke; the fourth was cosmetic.

SOMETIMES THE END of one story is the beginning of another. The deep-sea submersible *Alvin* released its weights on July 21, 1986, and said goodbye to the ocean floor. Steadily, inexorably, it began its ascent through two and a half miles of saltwater that pressed down with the weight of 6,000 pounds over every square inch of its titanium surface.

Safely sealed inside *Alvin's* belly, aliens from a world of air and light, pilot Ralph Hollis, graduate student Ken Stewart, and I watched through portholes and on video screens as the bottom of the Atlantic receded below us. There, centered in *Alvin's* floodlights, the stern of the Royal Mail Steamer *Titanic* grew smaller and smaller before fading out like a star swallowed by the darkness.

It was the eighth dive of our expedition to explore and photograph the remains of the legendary passenger ship. Other dives would follow—three more by this expedition and scores more in the years to come by salvagers, pirates, filmmakers, thrill-seekers, and even a New York couple who exchanged their wedding vows inside a submersible perched on the bow. But this trip, Dive No. 8, holds special significance for me. It was the last time I visited the R.M.S. *Titanic's* stern in person.

My team's discovery of the ship the previous year, with the help of French colleagues, had lit a bonfire of hysteria. We had thought that finding the ship, last seen sliding under the black waters of the icy North Atlantic in 1912, would do much to quench the public's insatiable curiosity. In fact, just

DOWN TO THE GREAT SHIP, *the search vehicle* Argo *starts its descent to* Titanic *in 1985.*

the opposite was true. The cottage industry that turns out books, films, television programs, newspaper and magazine articles, and memorabilia on *Titanic* continues to grow. It bears witness to the world's apparently unending fascination with the tragedy. We want to know every detail of its sinking, the life-and-death dramas on its decks and in its lifeboats, the official and unofficial inquiries that have attempted to apportion blame and to ask "what if." And we face the difficult issues of deciding the fate of *Titanic* now that the famous ocean liner is again connected to the human world.

TITANIC RESTS ON the Atlantic sea bottom, one thousand miles east of Boston, Massachusetts. The ship lies broken in the grave, its two main pieces connected by two overlapping debris fields. Yet if not for being buried in mud that rises 60 feet up its hull, the bow looks as if it could rise and sail again. It has magic and majesty. It is easy to imagine long-dead characters coming to life and acting out the ship's final hours.

More than nine decades ago, it was there, in the crow's nest high above the deck, that Frederick Fleet rang his warning bell three times at 11:40 p.m. on Sunday, April 14, and shouted, "Iceberg, right ahead!" into the ship's telephone. It was there, on the bridge, as the great ship barrelled along at

22 knots, that First Officer William Murdoch ordered "Hard a-starboard!" to Quartermaster Robert Hitchens, who spun the ship's telemotor wheel and tried to slip the ship safely around the danger. It was there, on the starboard side, that a mountain of ice hammered holes in the plates of *Titanic*'s first five compartments, erroneously labeled "watertight." The bow filled slowly with water and sank virtually unmolested by the forces of nature. It glided to the bottom. The impact, while enough to plant it firmly in the seabed, did not ruin its appearance.

Not so the stern. As the weight of water pouring into *Titanic*'s forward compartments dropped the bow, the brilliantly lighted stern rose free. Historian Walter Lord likened the lopsided, crippled ship to "a sagging birthday cake." Drawn by instinct for self-preservation, most of the some 1,500 people still on board clambered up the sloping decks toward the stern. They gathered, frightened, at the edge of the poop deck, which rose so high that the ship's propellers emerged from the Atlantic. The hull began to crack under strains it had never been designed to endure, and *Titanic* broke in two.

As the bow began its descent into the abyss, the stern slowly rotated upright and became the scene of almost unimaginable pathos. Loved ones said goodbye. Screams rang out in the clear night air. Some unfortunates jumped to their deaths. Others rode the ship down. Nearly 700 survivors

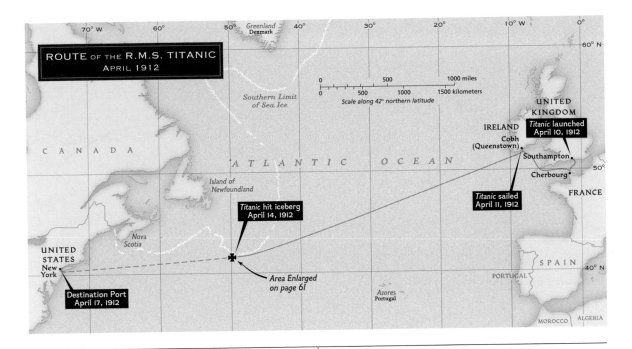

ROUTE OF THE **R.M.S. TITANIC**
APRIL 1912

Southern Limit of Sea Ice

ATLANTIC OCEAN

CANADA

Island of Newfoundland

Nova Scotia

UNITED STATES
New York

Titanic hit iceberg April 14, 1912

Area Enlarged on page 61

Destination Port April 17, 1912

UNITED KINGDOM

IRELAND
Cobh (Queenstown)

Titanic launched April 10, 1912

Southampton

Cherbourg

Titanic sailed April 11, 1912

FRANCE

SPAIN

PORTUGAL

Azores Portugal

MOROCCO | ALGERIA

Greenland Denmark

in lifeboats watched in horror. Of all who went with the stern into the freezing water, only a few dozen survived. The stern was a grim and terrible place to be at 2:20 a.m. on Monday, April 15, 1912.

Unlike the bow, the stern was not pressure-compensated. Large pockets of air remained trapped as the stern sank deeper and the ocean squeezed tighter. Steel plates bent, buckled, and finally imploded. The wrecked hulk plummeted. It struck the ocean floor like a bullet, flattening upon impact before suffering a second hammer blow, caused by the downdraft of its wake. One-inch steel plates peeled back like the lid of a sardine can. The decks themselves sandwiched upon each other, pressing ceilings and floors together as if the stern contorted to match the human agony.

Our 1986 expedition to *Titanic* began with the bow. That was the first section we had discovered a year earlier, when photographs and video taken by our vehicles *Argo* and *ANGUS* revealed the shipwreck to the world. We didn't locate the stern until many weeks later, when we pored over thousands of photographic images and pinpointed it about a half mile south of the bow.

SAILING FROM *Southampton to New York, map above,* Titanic *skirted a fateful ice field.*
THE BOW, *following pages, left, drips with rust in 1986 and, right, cuts a majestic profile on a 1912 postcard.*

MUG SHOT *of the prime suspect: An iceberg photographed shortly after* Titanic's *sinking may have been the killer.*

It wasn't until the eighth dive that we ventured toward the stern. We dropped in from high above instead of landing nearby and scooting through the debris across the ocean floor. The poop deck loomed in the darkness. Its tangle of debris and cables made it too risky for a landing, so Ralph set us down on the muddy bottom near the wall of the stern. Icicles of rust, which I christened "rusticles" (a name that seems to have caught on), covered all trace of the letters that formed the word *Titanic* on the steel above us. Our remote eyes—cameras in a tethered robot named *Jason Jr.*, or *J.J.*—were of no use to us. A malfunctioning motor had fouled our controls. To see the stern up close, Ralph piloted *Alvin* across the mud and under the overhanging bulk of the stern. We were gambling with our lives. If *Alvin* should suddenly develop a maneuvering glitch, we would not be able to rise straight up to the surface. The decks of the *Titanic*, above us, would catch and trap us.

Fortunately, *Alvin* performed perfectly. We moved close enough to view the stern's sloping steel plates. Buried in a ridge of mud were the ship's three propellers and all but 16 feet of its massive rudder. Ralph eased *Alvin* out from under the overhang and prepared to ascend. One last task remained.

In respect and honor, I planned on leaving something behind, a bronze memorial plaque, and I wanted to place it on the stern in tribute both to Bill Tantum, a friend in the Titanic Historical Society who had shared my dream of exploring the ship but died before its realization, and to all who perished on that icy night in 1912.

I had first thought of putting it on the bow, which looked much as it always had. But then I thought of the stern and all of its ghosts. If we were to honor their memory, the stern, where they had clung to life until the final moment, would be the proper place. Ralph piloted *Alvin* to the edge of the poop deck and parked it with its back end hanging into space. The submersible's mechanical arm gently deposited the plaque in the sediment dusting the hull. "In memory of those souls who perished with the 'Titanic,' April 14-15, 1912," it begins. Tears filled my eyes as we said goodbye and ascended. There would be three more dives by *Alvin,* but no moment matched the poignancy of that departure from the stern.

I knew when my first *Titanic* story ended in 1986 that I would not return in *Alvin* and would never again touch the ship. "I hope someday to lead a new expedition to the *Titanic*'s grim North Atlantic gravesite," I wrote in 1995. "Only if I do, I will visit the wreck without ever leaving my surface ship and broadcast the pictures live around the world." A remotely controlled underwater imaging system would replace manned submersibles. *Alvin* had served us well, but an accident could have left people dead. When a robot falters on the ocean floor, an oceanographer files an insurance claim and buys or builds a replacement.

Technology grows ever more sophisticated. The years since my 1986 visit to *Titanic* have seen profound developments in robotics, computer science, satellite communications, digital photography, and deep-sea exploration techniques, not to mention the explosive growth of the Internet. That sense of immediacy I thought could never be duplicated now exists in abundance through the perfection of what I call "telepresence."

In my Connecticut office I can turn on the flat computer monitor behind my desk and watch the sun rise on the shores of Monterey Bay, California. Sometimes I view the bay's seabed on another computer. In real time, I watch the seaweed dance in the currents and the occasional sea lion frolic amid the kelp. Cameras, lights, and computer technology conjure the ocean floor on glowing screens thousands of miles away, and the distinction between "telepresent" reality and reality itself dims.

After my first inspection of *Titanic* on the ocean floor, I wrote that the ship wouldn't change much in my lifetime if left unmolested by treasure hunters. Much has happened in the intervening two decades. Salvage operations have removed more than 6,000 objects from the ship and its debris fields. Submersibles carrying salvagers and curiosity seekers have landed scores of times, perhaps weakening the deck plates and hastening the expansion of holes in floors and walls.

Nature has also taken its toll on the ship. A group of Canadian scientists estimates that the ubiquitous rusticles are sucking several hundred pounds of iron from the ship each day.

Alarmed at these swift changes, colleagues and I at the Institute for Exploration (IFE) began devising a plan to use the newest technologies to map the *Titanic* site. High-definition still and video cameras would provide detailed pictures for scientific investigation of the ship's vertical hull surfaces, horizontal decks, and debris fields. Comparisons with similar views taken in 1985 and 1986 would document the deterioration of the ship and provide a baseline for future efforts to slow, stop, or perhaps even to reverse the vessel's decay. The *Titanic* might become the crown jewel of telepresence— a museum with cameras, lights, and other equipment installed to send images of the Grand Staircase, boat deck, and other features around the world.

A PLAQUE, *now gone, honors* Titanic *victims and historian Bill Tantum. The words are unclear due to imaging technology in 1986. Still, it shines in submarine* Alvin's *lights.*

If we were to reach that long-term goal— using today's advanced technology to rescue *Titanic,* in a sense—there would be an irony involved. The sinking of the great ocean liner awakened the world with a jolt. The tragic news overturned the American people's confidence about the future and left the national spirit moving, according to 17-year-old survivor Jack Thayer, "at a rapidly accelerating pace ever since, with less and less peace, satisfaction, and happiness. Today the individual has to be contented with rapidity of motion, nervous emotion, and economic insecurity. To my mind," wrote young Thayer, "the world of today awoke April 15th, 1912."

Faith in technology had set the stage.

DURING THE LATE 19th century, turbine-propelled steamships established an admirable record for safety. Whereas Dr. Samuel Johnson a century earlier characterized sea travel as "being in jail with the chance of being drowned," by the 1900s transatlantic passenger ships were like spacious and gracious hotels. British, French, German, and American shipping lines competed for lucrative fares with faster ships and greater luxuries. Most passengers traveled third class, or "steerage." Those who could afford the finer things, however, enjoyed elegant accommodations, sumptuous meals, and charming companions.

Line—needed to counter the new, swift ships introduced by the competing Cunard Line. White Star had nothing to match the *Lusitania* and *Mauretania,* swift ocean liners designed with the help of the British admiralty, that had been launched the previous year. White Star, which was owned by the genius of American capitalism, Junius Pierpont Morgan, lacked the economic

"WE WENT TO THE RAIL AND LOOKED OUT INTO THE BLACKNESS AHEAD.... I WENT TO MY BERTH THINKING OF THE PAINS AND TERRORS OF THOSE DOOMED TWO THOUSAND, A GREAT RAGE IN MY HEART AGAINST THE FORTUITY OF LIFE."
—THEODORE DREISER, ABOARD THE NEARBY *KROONLAND,* HAVING NEARLY BOARDED THE *TITANIC*

Bigger, better, and faster became the mantra of passenger ship construction. Under these circumstances, the idea that would become the *Titanic* was hatched on a summer evening in 1907 over Havana cigars and Napoleon brandy at the London home of Lord Pirrie, head of Harland & Wolff shipbuilders. J. Bruce Ismay, managing director of the Oceanic Steamship Navigation Company—popularly known as the White Star

concessions and naval expertise that the British government had poured into Cunard. Pirrie and Ismay, sipping their liquor, decided they could not outrun Cunard's ships. Instead, they would build ships for White Star unrivaled in luxury and size. As the night wore on and the two men doodled and discussed, they drew up plans for three sister ships: *Olympic, Titanic,* and *Gigantic.*

Within six months, the first of the three, *Olympic*, had its keel laid at Harland & Wolff's Belfast yard. *Titanic*'s keel followed, on March 31, 1909. The two ships took up three berths at Harland & Wolff. Each was 50 percent larger than any ship ever built. Both weighed in at 45,000 tons displacement, more than 12,000 tons heavier than *Lusitania* and *Mauretania*. Both were planned at 882 feet long, stretching more than 120 feet beyond the new Cunard liners, but the *Titanic* gained nine inches during construction, the world's longest ship at that time.

Titanic's design, along with sheer size, gave rise to the speculation that even God could not sink her and her sisters. Bulkheads that crossed from port to starboard separated her interior into 16 watertight compartments. Watertight doors, electrically controlled, were supposed to isolate flooding, and even if a right-angle collision filled two compartments with water, the ship could float. As the technical journal *Shipbuilder* reported in 1911, "The Captain may, by simply moving an electric switch, instantly close the doors throughout and make the vessel practically unsinkable." So much for hubris.

Edward J. Smith, 59, traditionally skippered White Star Line ships on their maiden voyages.

FALLEN WITNESS *to tragedy, a lifeboat davit, center, lies next to the toppled mast of* Titanic *in this 1986 view of the forward port section of the boat deck.*

He inspired confidence and commanded a loyal following of the rich and famous, earning him the nickname "the millionaires' captain." Crewmen noted how well he negotiated tight turns in harbors and appreciated his fairness despite his edgy quest for perfection. He appeared gruff and powerful, with a barrel chest and General Grant beard, yet Smith had an easy charm. "He was a great favorite, and a man any officer would give his ears to sail under," recalled Second Officer Charles Herbert Lightoller.

Smith planned to retire after completing the *Titanic*'s first round trip. He had confidence in the safety of his ships. Six years earlier, upon the first voyage of the White Star Line's *Adriatic*, a smaller passenger ship, he said he could not imagine what would make such a ship founder: "Modern shipbuilding has gone beyond that."

If the *Titanic* was twice as big as the *Adriatic*, it must be twice as safe. If damaged, it would serve as its own lifeboat. That's what Bruce Ismay believed—as, to his credit, he told the British Board of Trade inquiry after the sinking. Logic dictated that *Titanic* would float long enough to allow passengers to be rescued. Other vessels, notably the *Arizona* in 1879, had crashed into ice and survived. But the world must have appeared safer in 1912, when ships were not only bigger but also able to communicate over long distances at the speed of light. Rescue was only a matter of calling fellow captains via "wireless telegraphy."

Hence *Titanic* had ridiculously little lifeboat capacity. The White Star Line put 16 regulation lifeboats aboard, 8 on each side of the deck, along with 4 so-called Englehardt lifeboats, smaller vessels with collapsible canvas sides, stored upside down and released after other lifeboats had been lowered. *Titanic* carried about 2,200 on its maiden voyage, and the lifeboats and collapsibles had room for 1,178—more than the number required by British shipping regulations, which followed an outdated safety formula and required lifeboat seats for 962. *Titanic*'s only safety drill was rudimentary at best: two lifeboats lowered on sailing day. Passengers received no instruction on how to respond in an emergency. When Sylvia Caldwell boarded in Southampton, a deck hand told her, "God himself could not sink this ship."

The passengers who joined Mrs. Caldwell on board *Titanic* on April 10, 1912, represented a who's who of the Western world. The maiden voyage boasted passengers with a collective wealth of $250 million—an astonishing sum in 1912. The richest was Col. John Jacob Astor, immensely wealthy by virtue of his parlaying a family fortune in fur trading into a network of hotels and real estate. His new and pregnant wife, Madeleine, an 18-year-old he had married after a scandalous divorce, accompanied him.

Streetcar magnate George Widener and his family were aboard. His wife, Eleanor, had packed a million-dollar set of pearls. Also aboard was Benjamin Guggenheim, mining industry captain; Sir Cosmo and Lady Duff Gordon, British blue bloods; Macy's department store owner Isidor Straus and his wife, Ida; and John B. Thayer, the second vice president of the Pennsylvania Railroad and father to young Jack. First-class passenger Billy Carter of Philadelphia was rich enough not only to own a motorcar, a fashionable 35-horsepower Renault, but also to ship it across the Atlantic in the hold. Like many others in first class, Carter took much with him, including 24 polo sticks, 60 shirts, and 15 pairs of shoes.

Representing those who owned and built the ship on board were Ismay and Thomas Andrews, managing director of the Harland & Wolff Shipyard and the ship's builder. The former was on hand to see to the White Star's interests, the latter to find and correct any problems.

The most luxurious suite aboard *Titanic* booked for the equivalent of $4,200 one way across the Atlantic—several years' salaries for

SISTERS Olympic, *right, and* Titanic *take shape in a specially designed gantry, which stood in Belfast until 1973.*

those who toiled as its crew. (Third-class fare was $36.) For their money, passengers received every luxury that White Star had banked on to beat the competition. First-class passengers enjoyed such pleasures as a Turkish bath, a gymnasium with the most modern exercise equipment, a swimming pool, a darkroom, three elevators, fine restaurants, smoking rooms, and a squash court. European chefs offered exquisite fare. The luncheon menu on the final day afloat included grilled mutton chops, baked jacketed potatoes, salmon mayonnaise, Norwegian anchovies, and corned ox tongue.

The showpiece of public areas was the Grand Staircase, between the first and second funnels, or smokestacks. Natural light entering through a white-enameled glass dome bathed the stairs' polished balustrades and an elaborate clock, carved with figures representing Honor and Glory crowning Time. First-class staterooms seemed like palaces, with full-sized wrought-iron beds and washstands offering hot and cold water. Exclusive suites included their own private promenades.

CAPT. EDWARD J. SMITH, *right, and Purser Herbert W. McElroy stand near the officers' quarters on* Titanic's *boat deck. Both died, with some 700 other crew members.*

Second- and third-class accommodations, while not nearly as opulent, still outshone the typical rooms aboard *Titanic*'s competitors, thanks to comfortable beds, practical bathrooms, and good food. Like other ships of its day, *Titanic* did isolate third-class passengers, following U.S. laws that restricted the movement of immigrants.

Except for a near-collision as it got under way, caused by suction from its gigantic wake, *Titanic*'s first days proved uneventful. Passengers boarded at Southampton, England, then the ship crossed the channel for more fares at Cherbourg, France. From there it went on to Queenstown, Ireland, and to sea, bound for New York.

Other than a series of reports of ice in the North Atlantic, beginning with another ship's wireless message at sunset on April 12, and some confusion about missing binoculars for the lookouts, the voyage suggested a polished routine. The crew handled reports of ice ahead with a nonchalance that bordered on the cavalier. Captain Smith gave the first report to Fourth Officer Joseph Boxhall, who marked the ice field's location in the chart room. A thousand miles away and to the north, the ice offered no immediate threat. *Titanic* steamed on. The next night, another ship gave another report of ice. The *Rappahannock* had dented her bow and twisted her rudder in a collision with pack ice. *Titanic,* close enough to communicate by blinkered signal, acknowledged the message and sailed on.

During the next day, Sunday, April 14, *Titanic* received six more reports of ice directly in its path. The ship's crew treated them as insignificant. One warning, containing the jotted word "ice," got tucked like a shopping list into a frame in the chart room.

Captain Smith took another radioed warning, this one from the *Baltic,* and shoved it in his pocket. Instead of giving it to anyone on the bridge, where it might have done some good, he handed it to Ismay when the two men bumped into each other on the promenade deck. Ismay produced it at lunch to impress his dining

THE GRAND STAIRCASE, *featuring Louis XIV balustrades, descended to the first-class entrance on D deck.*

companions. That night, Ismay returned the note to Smith shortly before they went to dinner, but there's no evidence that the *Baltic*'s message ever made its way to the bridge.

Nobody systematically assembled the information from all the ice reports coming in. In the absence of an accurate chart, the *Titanic* crew believed that the most significant ice fields lay to the north of their track. In fact, they were sailing into a band of icebergs, sheet ice, and growlers, or small bergs, stretching 78 miles across. Thinking that only a few icebergs or growlers lay ahead, the crew steamed onward at nearly top speed.

On the last night of the voyage, one of Ismay's dining companions suggested that the ice warning he had produced from his pocket surely implied that the crew would slow the ship down. On the contrary, Ismay responded. "We'll be going all the faster to get by it. Put the trouble behind us as quickly as possible, that's what I always say."

Ismay knew the tradition: Ships typically traveled at full speed until an iceberg actually came into view. Such was the confidence in

LIFEBOATS *sit in their chocks on* Titanic's *uppermost deck. In addition to 16 wooden-sided boats, the ship had 4 canvas-sided "collapsibles," designed to fit into the davits. If every seat had been filled in all 20 boats, about half of those aboard would have been saved.*

LOST AT SEA *were industrialist Benjamin Guggenheim, top, and journalist W. T. Stead. Guggenheim put on white tie and tails to meet his death, stating, "No woman shall be left aboard this ship because Ben Guggenheim was a coward." Stead settled into an armchair to die.*

Titanic, its crew, and its technology. Any danger could be spotted in time and avoided; any inadvertent bumps along the way would not damage the greatest of all ships.

Weather conditions worked against the crew that night. The North Atlantic became so calm, it resembled a pool of oil. If only a breeze had kicked up a little chop, waves would have broken against the fatal iceberg and made it easier to see. The night air was so clear that *Titanic* seemed suspended in the center of a sphere of lights. The perfect reflection of stars in the water's surface made the horizon, and any icebergs that might break its even line, difficult to pick out.

At 11:40 p.m., lookout Frederick Fleet spotted something darker than the surrounding darkness. It looked no bigger than two tables shoved together, he later testified. But soon he recognized it for what it was: a mountain of ice, looming higher than the ship's forecastle. Fleet called it a "black mass." Sailors know that an iceberg can flip over as it melts, turning its underside to the air and becoming a dark-blue "black iceberg." When Fleet spotted the berg, it was only a third of a mile in front of the ship. First Officer William Murdoch reacted swiftly to his warning, but a 46,000-ton ship traveling at 21 knots takes about a mile to turn. Thirty-seven seconds after Fleet saw it, the iceberg scraped *Titanic*'s starboard side.

Survivors testified that the impact did not seem like much: "a dull thump," "just a little vibration," "like rolling over a thousand marbles." The injury was not so dramatic as a head-on collision nor so vicious as a gigantic open wound. But it proved fatal.

Captain Smith ran to the bridge from his nearby cabin and heard the news from Murdoch. The captain ordered the watertight doors closed, but Murdoch already had taken that precaution. He dispatched Boxhall and then Andrews, the shipbuilder, to assess the damage. Andrews found water pouring into the mailroom and gurgling against the squash court's backboard. Jack Thayer, dressed in pajamas and an overcoat, chanced upon Andrews shortly after midnight and learned the worst from the man most qualified to know: "He did not give the ship much over an hour to live," recalled Thayer. "We could hardly believe it, and yet if he said so, it must be true."

Titanic's fate was a simple matter of physics and geometry. The much-ballyhooed watertight compartments were no such thing. The bulkheads stood barely 15 feet above the waterline. As the ocean filled the fifth compartment, the weight dragged the bow low enough for water to slop over the top of the bulkhead and into the sixth. When the sixth filled, it flooded the seventh, and so on in a chain reaction, like filling an ice cube tray from one end with the spillover flowing toward the other.

Andrews's estimate of an hour was a bit off. *Titanic* floated for just over two and a half hours

FORTUNES DIVERGED *among survivors. Socialite Margaret Brown, top, became "Unsinkable Molly," while the press pilloried White Star Managing Director J. Bruce Ismay for not going down with his ship. He is shown above, at right, with his attorney.*

M

EN, GET ON YOUR LIFE BELTS, THERE'S TROUBLE AHEAD!" a *Titanic* officer ordered the denizens of the first-class Smoking Room shortly after midnight on April 15, 1912. Few looked up from drinks and cards. Why should they? Logic dictated that the ship could not be in any danger.

Many changed their attitudes and put on their life jackets as *Titanic* slowly dropped into the 28°F ocean water. John Jacob Astor reassured his young, pregnant wife about the canvas jackets by slicing one open to show her the cork inside. Madeleine Astor put on her jacket and survived in a lifeboat, while her husband went into the water and was crushed when the forward funnel fell on him.

Passenger Helen Candee knew the fate awaiting those in life jackets who did

THE LIFE JACKET

not secure a lifeboat seat. Assuming the worst when she saw a procession of people wearing "the sinister emblem of death at sea," Candee described the crowded scene on deck as "a fancy-dress ball in Dante's hell." While life jackets could keep people from drowning, they offered no shield against bitter cold. Hypothermia killed most of those who entered the Atlantic. The life jacket above was taken from a body recovered at the *Titanic* site by the crew of the *Mackay-Bennett*. The body was one of 116 later buried at sea.

If any good could be said to have emerged from that terrible night, it can be found in *Titanic*'s impact on maritime safety laws. Ice patrols began reporting all contacts with bergs, radio operators stayed in constant communication, and archaic Board of Trade rules that governed lifeboat capacity were thoroughly overhauled. The new rule was simplicity itself: a seat for everyone aboard ship, period. Life jackets also remained a requirement.

before giving up the ghost. Those 160 minutes are a key reason its story remains so compelling. The time between collision and sinking allowed for a thousand dramatic moments as passengers and crew faced the prospect of their own deaths. There would be time for Ida Straus to refuse a seat held for her in a lifeboat and join her husband on the deck, saying, "We have been living together for many years. Where you go, I go."

There would be time for Jacob Astor to see his pregnant wife into Lifeboat No. 4 and then accept Lightoller's order preventing men from entering. There would be time for Guggenheim and his valet to change into evening clothes and prepare "to go down like gentlemen." There would be time for radio operator Jack Phillips to tap out one of the first SOS signals in maritime history, and to end his frantic communications with the musical symbol of death—the letter "V" twice in Morse Code, *dit-dit-dit da, dit-dit-dit-da,* the sound that Beethoven used in his *Fifth Symphony* to portray the Grim Reaper's knocking. There would be time for the lights of a mysterious ship to appear on the horizon and offer a glimmer of hope, only to disappear again. There would be time for the orchestra to assemble on deck and play calmly amid the chaos.

None of the musicians would survive. Likewise, Andrews would die, standing stunned and statuelike in the Smoking Room as the waters rushed over the decks. Captain Smith, First Officer Murdoch, and most of the crew would join them, as would radio operator Phillips.

In all, 678 members of the crew perished; 212 survived. Among the passengers, the death ratio was lowest in first class, where survivors actually outnumbered the fatalities. Death rang up a high score in third class, where ship's barriers, the passengers' many languages, and a mixture of neglect and ignorance meant that three quarters of them perished. Despite official orders that the lifeboats should be filled with "women and children first," the loss rate for third-class children was higher than that for first-class men. Twenty-nine third-class female passengers died for every dog carried by a first-class passenger into a lifeboat. Many third-class passengers, as well as crewmen laboring in the engine rooms, remained trapped in the hull as the ship sank. Their bodies likely are still there on the ocean floor, kept from dissolving by the nearly oxygen-free waters walled off from the surrounding ocean.

Many of those able to escape to the upper decks went down with the stern. Regardless of whether they wore life jackets, nearly all died. Few had the chance to drown. Falling into frigid water of 28°F (lower than the usual freezing point

SURVIVORS *in the crowded Collapsible D, following pages, left, approach the rescue ship* Carpathia. *A day later, right, a London newsboy peddles the headlines.*

because of the abundance of salt), the victims met swift deaths by hypothermia.

In the end, about 700 people survived, most pulled from lifeboats several hours later by the rescue ship *Carpathia,* which came in answer to Phillips's wireless summons. Ismay, the White Star's ranking representative, would be condemned for his decision to take a seat in Collapsible C rather than go down with the ship. He turned his back and hid his head as the great ship vanished, unable to witness the horror. On board the *Carpathia,* he sequestered himself in a physician's cabin and received no visitors except for Jack Thayer, who found Ismay "completely wrecked" and virtually catatonic. He remained medicated on opiates, unable to eat or communicate until the *Carpathia* reached New York.

T ITANIC SANK ROUGHLY one thousand miles east of Boston. There it remained, undisturbed by human attention, for 73 years, 4 months, and 17 days.

Not for lack of interest, however. The bereaved, the curious, and even the downright loony took turns dreaming of ways to find or raise the ship. The first to discuss the idea of locating the *Titanic* probably was Vincent Astor, son of the dead tycoon. Within days of the tragedy, he proposed exploding the ship's hull as a way to release the body of his father, which he believed to be still inside. When the millionaire's corpse turned up the next day, the younger Astor dropped the idea.

Later in 1912, the surviving Astors, Wideners, and Guggenheims determined to let their money talk. They contracted with a wrecking company to find and raise the hull, but the inadequate technology of the time quickly demonstrated that there are some things money can't buy. Still, the deep thinkers of the age knew that the day would come when technology would work miracles. In 1914 a *Popular Mechanics* article about photography predicted that the children of *Titanic*'s dead would one day see pictures of the wreck.

As the years passed, schemes for raising the ship included passing over the hull in a submarine equipped with electromagnets; attaching pontoons filled with helium or gasoline to it; and filling the hull itself with wax, ice, or some other lighter-than-water substance. But none of these plans involved an all-important step: First find the *Titanic,* then worry about what to do with it.

The first serious expedition occurred in 1953. The British salvage firm of Risdon Beasley sailed to the place its investigators thought was the wreck site. *Titanic*'s last position, as worked out by Fourth Officer Boxhall and transmitted by radio operator Phillips, lay at latitude 41°46' N, longitude 50°14' W. Steaming nearby, Risdon Beasley set off a series of underwater explosives. The salvage crew aimed to paint an echo-picture of the ocean bottom. Their technique contained the seeds of more sophisticated sonar imaging available at century's end, but it came to naught. We now know that *Titanic* lies in a canyon nearly 13,000 feet below the surface. Under those conditions, zeroing in on the ship's outline with crude explosive echoes was like trying to shoot skeet with a howitzer.

Others would try, without success, in the coming years. A Texas oil tycoon, Jack Grimm, plagued his operations from the beginning. He wanted to play hunches, but his scientific team preferred a systematic approach. Grimm paid the bills, so he won that battle—but lost the war. The best he could do was to announce the location of something that may have been a propeller—and then fail to provide any proof.

In fact, Grimm's expeditions missed the hull of *Titanic* completely, coming no closer than one

"WE SAW THE BODY OF ONE WOMAN DRESSED ONLY IN HER NIGHT DRESS, CLASPING A BABY TO HER BREAST."

—JOHANNA STUNKE, ABOARD THE *BREMEN*, WHICH PASSED CLOSE BY THE SITE OF THE SINKING

bankrolled an ambitious search in the early 1980s. Grimm had made a name for himself by seeking the mythical Noah's Ark, Loch Ness monster, and Bigfoot. On his three *Titanic* expeditions from 1980 to 1983, he had state-of-the-art scientific equipment, crackerjack brains to operate it, and the certainty that this quarry was real.

Grimm also had a reputation for good fortune, but it deserted him in the North Atlantic. Bad weather, bad luck, and confusion about where and how to conduct a search and a half miles to the site we can now identify. And yet his failure was instructive. Grimm had used some of the finest oceanographic equipment available on his second and third expeditions, including the Deep Tow side-scan sonar from San Diego's Scripps Institute of Oceanography. Deep Tow could give a fairly sharp sonar image of any large topographical feature on the ocean bottom, be it a rock formation or the upright wreck of a ship. It moves back-and-forth with its imaging system in a striped pattern called "mowing the lawn" by oceanographers. This creates a comprehensive survey of the ocean floor. But Grimm and his scientists never cut as much grass as they should have. They started with a fairly good idea of where the *Titanic* had settled. They hypothesized that Boxhall had erred in the coordinates he had given Phillips, failing to correct for the changing local time as the ship chased the sun west. They drew a rectangle on the map of the North Atlantic, siting *Titanic's* final radioed position near the lefthand side. If Grimm's team had had the time and the determination to scour the entire box they had drawn, they might have found the elusive prize, for *Titanic* actually rested just inside the edge of their search rectangle. But Grimm diverted his team from covering the entire "lawn" in favor of tracking a handful of intriguing sonar blips and guesses, leaving *Titanic* tantalizingly out of reach.

Actually finding the lost ship required analysis of two other shocking disasters at sea. The first was the implosion of the U.S.S. *Thresher,* a nuclear submarine, in April 1963. It

JASON JR. *examines* Titanic's *port bow during one of the 1986 explorations. The tether at right connects the unmanned robot to the submersible* Alvin.

was the height of the Cold War, and America worried over the threat of the Soviet Navy. *Thresher* had flown through an overhaul and a series of shakedown cruises at the Naval Shipyard in Portsmouth, New Hampshire. Although experts had their doubts about the reliability of its joints and pipes, the sub was rushed back to sea for a descent to the deepest point to which it was designed to go.

Somewhere east of New England, something went wrong. Investigators later concluded that a pipe probably broke. Highly pressurized water probably formed a fog inside the submarine, which in turn could have shorted out an electrical panel and set off a chain of events that shut down the power to its fission reactor. Too deep to blow the conventional ballast tanks and rise through buoyancy, the sub required a hot reactor to turn its propellers and fly to the surface. Instead, *Thresher* apparently stalled and drifted backward and down. A monitoring post aboard a surface ship heard the words "test depth" from below, then an explosion. *Thresher* and all 129 aboard went to the bottom.

Inspection of *Thresher*'s wreckage to learn from the disaster posed the same problem that had plagued early attempts to locate *Titanic*. The submarine lay under 5,400 feet of water—not even half the depth of *Titanic*, but deep enough to be hard to pinpoint. At first, the Navy tried to drop cameras on tethers. Since they did not know the exact location of the wreck, they might as well have been tossing darts blindfolded. So the job was handed to divers in the bathysphere *Trieste*, at the time the only vehicle designed to take humans that far down underwater. Despite

Trieste's ungainly shape, tiny windows, and lack of mobility, it located the wrecked submarine.

The Navy declared success, but the truth was not so black and white. *Trieste* had found neither *Thresher*'s reactor nor its containment vessel, nor had it mapped the sub's debris field. In order to learn more and lay to rest concern over radiation leaks, the Navy had to develop a new generation of deep-sea exploration vehicles.

Technological leaps do not happen overnight. Five years after the *Thresher*'s demise, a second submarine disaster underscored the need for

WITH JEAN-LOUIS MICHEL, *far right, in 1985, I watch, arms folded,* Titanic *on* Knorr's *video screens.*

deep-sea submersibles. On May 21, 1968, the U.S.S. *Scorpion* mysteriously sank 400 miles south of the Azores in the eastern Atlantic. Details of *Scorpion*'s accident remained classified until the 1990s, after the collapse of the Soviet Union ended the Cold War. Theories conflict, but two scenarios suggest that it sank because of a faulty torpedo or an explosion in a battery compartment. Darker rumors hint that perhaps a common game of cat-and-mouse resulted in a Soviet torpedo sending the *Scorpion* to its grave—although I've seen the Navy's declassified reports and discount those rumors as the work of wild-eyed conspiracy theorists. Nevertheless, there has never been enough evidence gathered from the *Scorpion* wreck to reach ironclad conclusions. Like *Thresher, Scorpion* was just too deep to examine up close at the time. It lies broken in half, 11,500 feet underwater. Unlike its sister sub, though, a greater urgency drove its examination, for *Scorpion* contained not only a reactor full of radioactive materials but also two nuclear-tipped Mark 45 Astor torpedoes.

In 1969, the Navy sent the submersible *Trieste II* to investigate. It found no evidence of an external torpedo explosion, but it could not enter the sub for a closer look. That assignment called for a small, tethered, unmanned robot. It would require fiber-optic technology, coming into common use in the late 1970s and early 1980s, to transmit high-quality images to a surface ship. It would need a finely tuned maneuvering system. And the surface ship at the other end of the tether, where observers would send commands and collect data, would have to have a dynamic positioning system to stay directly above the robot and keep the tether slack.

I had the initial idea for creating just such an observation system while I was on sabbatical at Stanford University from 1979 to 1980. The Navy gave me the green light to develop it in 1982. At the time the Cold War was still in full swing, and concerns about controlling the possible battleground of the ocean bottom made the need seem obvious. Money came from the Office of Naval Research.

The team responsible for creating the remotely operated vehicle (ROV) system assembled at Woods Hole, Massachusetts, where I had my office at the time. I put together the Deep Submergence Laboratory there to dream, to think, and then to build. The brains working on the ROV system included some of the most brilliant in marine science and imaging technology. Sparking off each other's ideas, they began drawing up not one vehicle, but two: *Argo* and *Jason*.

In Greek mythology, the ship *Argo* sailed with a crew of Argonauts to fetch the Golden Fleece; Jason was the handsome, brave admiral who led the expedition through many dangers to ultimate success. In our modern parallel, *Argo* would descend from the surface ship and search the ocean floor until it found something worth closer examination. Then it would dispatch intrepid little *Jason* with its lights, camera array, and fiber-optic leash to fetch modern science's equivalent of the Golden Fleece: a mountain of data.

In the summer of 1984, while *Jason* was still in development, *Argo* was ready for a test. Its first target: *Thresher*. The Navy wanted to map the debris and ascertain whether the ship or its missing reactor was leaking radiation. The system worked like a charm.

ONE OF TITANIC'S *two reciprocating engines stands proud in 1986 while decks at its right have collapsed. The nearly 40-foot-tall engines were the largest of their kind ever built.*

Aboard the surface ship *Knorr,* we "mowed the lawn" over the wreckage, taking enough pictures to demonstrate *Argo*'s value. What the photos revealed was even more instructive. *Thresher*'s reactor had plowed straight down into the muddy bottom at nearly a hundred miles per hour. There it lay in its own crater, its radiation safely contained. Other debris lay in a curious pattern. Instead of forming a circle around the impact crater, like the blast of a shotgun, it had drifted in the currents. Light debris, such as a glove and a chart, had traveled far; heavier debris

not so far. The pattern resembled a comet and its tail. The explanation was simple. Like wind when a farmer winnows wheat, the current carried off the chaff and left the solid kernels. Any ship that sank in deep water would produce a similar debris field. *Argo* had found an essential key for finding shipwrecks: Crisscross the ocean floor looking for a debris field, then follow it like an arrow to the source.

In 1985, it was *Scorpion*'s turn. The Navy ordered a secret voyage to study the condition of the nuclear torpedoes and the cause of the sub's destruction. It was another test run for the fledgling *Argo,* and the Navy allocated three weeks for the project. If *Scorpion*'s condition could be detailed in less time, I would be allowed the remaining days for another, unofficial exploration I had planned.

By August 17, the *Knorr,* with a crew of 25 and a scientific team of 24, hovered above *Scorpion*. The sub had split in half near the ocean surface, and each part formed its own crater upon striking the ocean floor. The debris field fit the *Thresher* model perfectly: a comet tail ending with the main

PAINTED FOOTBOARD *from a first-class cabin bed remained untouched by time when encountered by* Alvin.

wreckage. Overall, *Scorpion* was in better condition than *Thresher,* but its hull prevented the close-up torpedo study the Navy had hoped for. No conclusive evidence emerged in the photographs to explain *Scorpion's* demise. (Several years later, the experts who originally investigated *Scorpion's* sinking learned that the Navy had issued a classified alert in 1968, shortly before the accident, red-flagging a design flaw that created a risk of torpedo battery explosion. This explanation best matches the appearance of *Scorpion's* wreckages.)

Complete mapping of the sub and its debris field took only four days. Mission accomplished—

although we could say little about it at the time. The *Knorr* and *Argo* had a date to keep in the mid-Atlantic, with the most famous ship of all time. I already had made plans with a French exploration team to pool our resources. The Institut Français de Recherche pour l'Exploitation de la Mer (IFREMER) had jumped at the chance to search for *Titanic.* Jean-Louis Michel led their team. To the French, who are among the world's best in undersea exploration techniques and technology, finding the *Titanic* ranked with the first moon landing among landmarks of modern science. In midsummer they had combed the sea floor with a sensitive, side-scan sonar towed by the surface ship *Le Suroit.*

Titanic continued to prove elusive. Rough seas prevented *Le Suroit* and its sonar system from completely covering the ocean floor. There were gaps and shadows when the sonar veered off its intended path or too close to the ocean floor. The French team left, frustrated, on August 6, having covered only about 70 percent of the target area. *Knorr* arrived 18 days later with Michel on board as the chief representative of the French team. We had only 11 days before *Knorr* had to return to the States.

What to do? Michel and I went back to the beginning. We reexamined the historical data about *Titanic*'s sinking and drew a larger box on the map for our new search area. In addition, I applied the lessons of *Thresher* and *Scorpion*. *Titanic* passenger Jack Thayer had published in his eyewitness account that the ship had broken in half as its bow dipped and stern rose. If that were true, much of the ship's contents had spilled and spread on their journey to the ocean floor. *Titanic* would have a gigantic debris field, much larger than those of the submarines.

According to the log of another ship near *Titanic* as it sank, the surface current on April 15, 1912, moved south at 0.7 knots. Debris would scatter at least a mile along a north-south axis. Visual inspection would be our best bet. Towing *Argo* east to west above the ocean floor likely would intersect the north-south debris field. By following the crumbs, we would find *Titanic.*

We started five miles south of where *Carpathia* had found survivors in lifeboats. I never like to start a maritime archaeological search at the bull's-eye. Rather, I want to start at one side and then move closer. *Knorr* chugged steadily along at less than a walking pace, dragging *Argo* on a tether like a lead weight on a fishing line. For hours, days, nights, the images transmitted to *Knorr*'s control room showed mind-numbing sameness: blank, brown ocean bottom.

All that changed at 12:48 a.m., September 1. Metallic objects began to stream across the video monitors. The groggy crew snapped to attention and quickly verified that *Argo* had found a debris field of some kind. Shortly after 1 a.m., conclusive evidence appeared. A gigantic boiler, built to generate the steam that turned propellers, came into view. The crew whooped and hollered as Michel tracked down a photograph of *Titanic*'s engine room. It was a perfect match.

Within days, color pictures winged their way to major news media outlets. They fascinated the world and, unfortunately, drove a wedge between my team and IFREMER. Our plan had been for a simultaneous release on both sides of the Atlantic, but American television networks broadcast the images before the French had the chance to do so. IFREMER, understandably miffed, would not join us for a return trip.

The discovery in 1985 had been a quick and fortunate appendix to an expedition focusing on *Scorpion* as its main objective. It proved in a dramatic way that ROVs could explore the ocean floor. But the expedition had not explored the *Titanic* up close. The world had gone bananas over video and still pictures captured by *Argo* and its plain older sister, the film-camera sled *ANGUS* (Acoustically Navigated Geological Underwater Survey), but those images were just precursors of the ones yet to come.

That night, though, on the surface of the North Atlantic, shortly after 2 a.m. on September 1, 1985, our thoughts wandered far from the future excitement, sound, and fury our discovery would bring. Instead, we gathered at *Knorr*'s fantail and remembered another night long ago, two hours after midnight, in the same chilly waters. I raised the White Star Line flag of Harland & Wolff. The sky was clear, the sea's surface like glass. We held a brief memorial service, our elation replaced by reflection. Then, our moment of new beginnings behind us and a world of new challenges still ahead, I said to those assembled, "Thank you all. Now let's get back to work."

The work continues. ■

AT DIVE'S END, *in 1986, David Sanders and John Salzig secure safety lines to* Jason Jr.'s *garage before* Alvin *is raised aboard the deck of surface ship* Knorr.

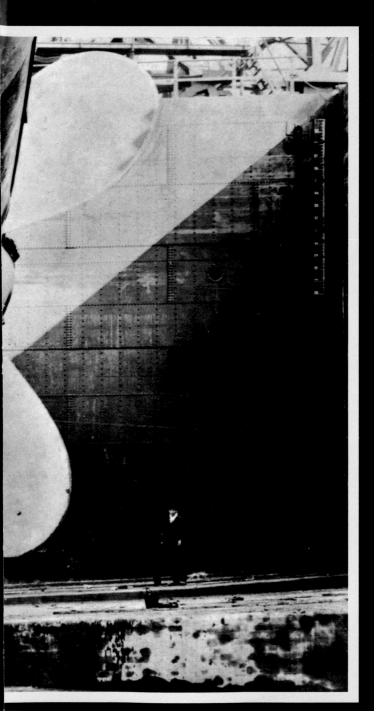

THE HISTORY

When the White Star Line conceived Titanic *and its two sister ships, its directors knew they could not compete against the Cunard liners* Lusitania *and* Mauretania *in speed. Instead, they asked Harland & Wolff to dwarf their rival's ships in size and luxury. In size,* Titanic *lived up to its name, as shown when a work crew, left, stood next to its 23-foot-wide, three-bladed propellers in the Belfast shipyard. For luxury,* Titanic *had a swimming pool, above, a squash court, Turkish bath, gymnasium, and the finest of restaurants.*

CAPT. E. J. SMITH *peers over the side near a lifeboat, above. This photo, and the one at right, were taken during the maiden voyage by Francis M. Browne, a candidate for the priesthood who got off at Queenstown, in Ireland.*

AT PLAY *on the first-class promenade deck, Robert Douglas Spedden, six years old, spins a top as his father, Frederic, watches. Both survived, as did the boy's mother, Daisy, and two servants. Frederic was allowed into Lifeboat No. 3 because no more women were at hand.*

TO SALVAGE *or* TO SAVE

BRONZE *blades of Titanic's starboard propeller resist the biological decay consuming the ship's iron.*

OLITICAL OBSERVERS call it a "feeding frenzy." Reporters sense big news lurking beneath the surface of daily routines. Metaphorically, it's blood in the water. Journalists cluster around the story like sharks, each swimming in to take a bite. Before 1985 most of my contact with the news media had been superficial. Thus I partly blame my own inexperience for the frenzy that burst as *Knorr* returned from its voyage of discovery.

When we set sail for Woods Hole after finding *Titanic,* my research team had been so caught up in the excitement of locating and photographing the wreck that we had not made detailed plans for releasing information. Wild rumors surfaced in the British press that we were actually trying to salvage the ship. Nobody knew then that *Titanic,* broken into pieces, could not be raised. Radio

broadcasts that reached us at sea reported protests against our supposed desecration of the wreckage. Nothing could have been further from the truth, and we had to get our version of the story out, even if it was fragmentary. Thus, when a helicopter from a Canadian television network lowered a cage to us as we stood on the deck of the *Knorr,* we gave the crew the first video of *Titanic*'s boiler on the ocean floor as well as footage of our predawn celebration on September 1. We provided three copies of everything, one for Woods Hole, one for IFRE-MER, and one for the world press, meaning every interested journalist. The chopper took off to the

A CRANE ABOARD *the French research ship* Suroit *in the North Atlantic prepares to launch a sonar search vehicle during the joint French-American expedition in 1985 that resulted in the discovery of* Titanic.

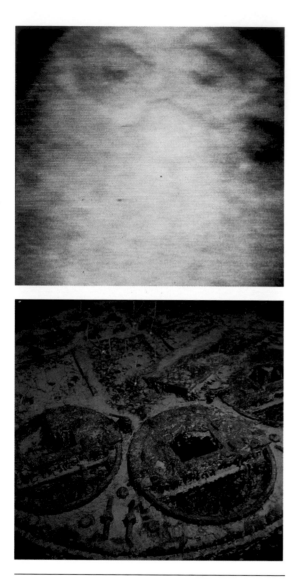

A TELLTALE PATTERN *of rivets and fire doors led to confirmation of* Titanic's *discovery when the top image appeared on* Knorr's *video monitors. Nineteen years later, the high-definition cameras of ROV Hercules rendered the same boiler in sharp detail, bottom.*

west, and we returned to our work, oblivious to the match we had just struck and held beneath the fuse. Storm winds kicked up 20-foot waves in the North Atlantic, but on shore the Labor Day weekend remained calm and quiet—the perfect time for *Titanic* to dominate print and broadcast media without competing news. The public got a taste of our story and demanded more.

CBS somehow got on the air first, describing its copy of the footage as "exclusive," despite our best efforts to share the images with the entire planet. The network's competitors, the have-nots, yowled in protest. They threatened to sue Woods Hole's administrators, who in turn radiophoned *Knorr* in a panic. With our French colleagues, I tried to draw up a new, more equitable arrangement to tell our story. That led to a second helicopter, chartered by the three major American networks, visiting *Knorr* at sea. Two couriers, a Frenchman and an American from the expedition, boarded the chopper with photos from *ANGUS*. The plan was simultaneous release in the United States and France, as befitting the international, cooperative venture.

Once again, our best-laid plans failed us. Network pressure made Woods Hole crack. American television went on the air with our newest photos while the package was still being delivered to our French friends. French TV producers refused to be scooped on a story involving Gallic pride and paid American sources for images via satellite. The mess helped cause a rupture

TO SALVAGE OR TO SAVE

between my team and IFREMER that had enormous consequences in years to come.

Knorr sailed into the harbor at Woods Hole on September 9. Someone fired a cannon in salute as we approached. A band struck up a lively tune, flags waved, and throngs lined the docks to greet us. Jean-Louis Michel, the expedition co-leader, and I gave our prepared remarks. My French colleague spoke first, explaining that the exploration of *Titanic* occurred "with her dignity in mind at all times." When my turn came, I praised my colleagues and the joint effort that found the ship. Exhausted and emotionally drained, I added: "The *Titanic* lies in 13,000 feet of water on a gently sloping alpinelike countryside overlooking a small canyon below. Its bow faces north and the ship sits upright on the bottom. There is no light at this great depth and little life can be found. It is a quiet and peaceful and fitting place for the remains of this greatest of sea tragedies to rest. May it forever remain that way and may God bless these found souls."

Forever is a long time. Although our return trips to *Titanic* respected the sanctity of the site, others have not always been so careful.

We came back in 1986 with the financial support of the U.S. Navy and a mission to test the newest tool of deep-sea exploration: the remotely operated vehicle *Jason Junior,* or *J. J.* It had no robotic arms or hands, as its larger successors would.

The second trip lacked some initial drama, to be sure, since we knew exactly where to sail. Out of port at Woods Hole in a different ship, *Atlantis II,* we churned 900 miles to the precise latitude and longitude. Seas and skies remained calm, but our spirits were touched by a gray melancholy. A chill had frosted our relations with the French, who felt snubbed by the news media snafus in 1985. Neither Michel nor the French submersible *Nautile* joined us this time.

As it neared the site, *Atlantis II* plunked three transponder beacons into the ocean floor to provide a tracking grid for our submersible voyages to the shipwreck. A transducer on the hull repeatedly pinged as we approached *Titanic*'s exact coordinates. Echoes from the ocean floor created a rather monotonous portrait in sound until we settled above the sonar silhouette of a sleeping giant. There, exactly where it should be, lay the great ship. We maneuvered *Atlantis II* into position and prepared our exploratory vehicles to go below.

We could not announce it at the time, but this first test for *Jason Jr.* served as a dress rehearsal for a secret Navy mission. An engineering team led by the Deep Submergence Laboratory's Chris von Alt had designed *J. J.* to fit into what we thought was an open hatch in the wreckage of *Scorpion,* hoping it could find clues as to why the sub sank or evidence of the fate of its nuclear-tipped torpedoes.

KNORR'S RETURN *in 1985, following pages, left, draws a crowd at Woods Hole. The voyage a year later to explore* Titanic *made even* Jason Jr. *a star, right.*

J. J. did not require a large bubble of breathable atmosphere, making it cheaper and smaller than a manned submersible. Its blue box, about the size of a power lawn mower, contained a tightly packed array of lights, cameras, and motors tucked inside a cube of positively buoyant syntactic foam. Like a dog on a leash, it could stick its nose into a dark space or explore interesting warrens deep inside a tangle of metal. With the Navy footing the bill, J. J.'s trip to *Titanic* was aimed to shake out any bugs in preparation for its more important mission to *Scorpion*. It had never been tested in the deep ocean.

J. J.'s neutrally buoyant tether was only 250 feet long. Its controllers—as if playing a million-dollar video game—sat inside the Navy's most trusted workhorse of the deep, *Alvin*. Built in 1964 to operate at depths of 6,000 feet, the submersible had been upgraded to a range of 13,000 feet, just enough to visit *Titanic*.

I was determined to be one of the three crew members in *Alvin* on the initial trip to the bow section. The nautical community was chuckling. Here I was, preparing to enter a submersible to visit *Titanic* in person despite my well-known comments that likened manned deep-sea craft to dinosaurs headed for extinction. I stood by my predictions (and still do), but the truth was that the next step in the

JASON JR., *attached by tether to the unseen* Alvin, *maneuvers with its thrusters to hover next to a window and peer into Stateroom U during the 1986 expedition.*

evolution of remotely operated vehicles, the powerful robot *Jason,* wasn't ready yet. *Jason Junior* fit inside *Alvin's* exterior garage and would ride there to the bottom of the ocean. Once unleashed on *Titanic,* the little ROV would take both video and still pictures. Marine scientist Elazar "Al" Uchupi had pored over the earlier photographs of *Titanic* and was on hand to analyze whatever images J. J. collected.

ONE SMALL STEP *initiates a journey to the bottom of the ocean as I prepare to enter the submersible* Alvin *through its red "sail."*

I joined my two most experienced submersible fliers, Ralph Hollis and Dudley Foster, for the initial dive. We took off our shoes and stepped inside *Alvin's* fiberglass turret at 8:15 a.m., July 13. Down we crawled into the spherical belly of the beast. Imagine three people buttoning themselves inside a single mechanical suit—this perfect little sphere was just six feet in diameter—and you have some idea of the constriction. The sub's rate of descent and ascent clocked in at just over one mile per hour. That would give us about two and a half hours to stare out the windows at the surrounding gloom, listen to music, and try not to think about how cramped we felt or about how much we might need to answer nature's call.

Ralph sealed us inside. An oxygen tank hissed and blew a musty stream of air, filling *Alvin* with the life-giving commodity we would need on the ocean floor. Meanwhile a lithium-hydroxide blower began scrubbing away exhaled carbon dioxide, preventing toxic buildup. At 8:35 a.m., we got the go-ahead from our surface controller to begin our descent, leaving the brilliant summer sun for the icy blackness. A jellyfish slid by my viewport, followed a few minutes later by a white-tipped shark, as if to advertise their natural adaptation to the world where we ventured as outsiders.

On descents, daylight left rapidly, and the ocean grew thicker overhead, until darkness ruled the universe. We always carried layers of clothes to put on as the icy cold penetrated *Alvin* and to take off as we returned to summer air and surface waves. For the several hours we were stuck inside the submersible, we kept away from contact with the hull, which was chilly from the surrounding water and slick with condensation from our breath. Classical music, typically Beethoven or Vivaldi, accompanied our descents. Return trips were the time for rock and roll. In between, while we navigated around the ocean floor, we went about our work in silence.

The first dive proved anything but routine. Halfway down, an alarm shrieked to notify us of seawater leaking into a battery pack aboard. We switched to a backup system, but it still meant a shortened visit to *Titanic*. There would be barely enough time to say hello before goodbye.

us north of our target, and began groping our way through the pitch darkness. Fortunately, by that time *Atlantis II* had reestablished the transponders' tracking system and alerted us by acoustic telephone that *Titanic* lay just to our right. Ralph steered *Alvin* along the ocean bottom. The gently rolling plain beneath us began to rise, until we were climbing a wall of mud that had been pushed

> "I AM RETURNING TO THE SITE TO SHOW THE WORLD A BETTER FUTURE FOR *TITANIC* THAN THE ONE SHE HAS SUFFERED.... PRIORITIES SHOULD NOT BE THE PLUNDERING OF THE PYRAMIDS OF THE DEEP, BUT INSTEAD THEIR LONG-TERM CARE AND APPRECIATION."
> —ROBERT D. BALLARD, 2004 *TITANIC* EXPEDITION

On the bottom we hit another snag. One of the floor-anchored transponders refused to provide *Atlantis II* with a strong signal, so our surface navigators could not tell us which way to pilot *Alvin* to find *Titanic*. The darkness is so complete, the lights so quickly scattered, that we could have been a few dozen feet from the ship and not have seen it. *Alvin* had its own sonar system, but it too had quit working. We turned the sub to face the current out of the south, on the assumption that it had pushed

up by *Titanic,* as if its impact had turned the sea bottom like some monstrous plow. Just as we knew that the ship must lie immediately ahead, *Alvin*'s alarm system indicated the battery leak had become critical. We were on sensory overload with tension and expectation.

Then we saw it.

Titanic's black steel skin seemed to stretch into infinity. It made me unconsciously hold my breath. The moment of triumph reminded me of Edmund

CQD . . . CQD . . . MGY . . . 41° 46 N, 50° 14 W . . . CQD . . . SOS." When Jack Phillips radioed *Titanic*'s first distress call, he tapped out CQ, meaning "all stations," with D for "distress." He followed that with *Titanic*'s call letters, MGY, and the latitude and longitude. A few minutes later, Harold Bride reminded Phillips that an international convention had chosen a new distress code, SOS. Phillips added those letters and kept sending.

Fourth Officer Joseph Boxhall had calculated *Titanic*'s latitude and longitude as precisely as he could, as lives depended on rescuers finding a tiny spot in a featureless ocean. But Boxhall figured wrong. He almost nailed the latitude, which could be calculated by measuring the angle of heavenly bodies above the horizon. Figuring longitude, however, required accurate data on elapsed time and ship's speed.

POSITION AT SEA

Titanic's speed probably was below 21 knots. Boxhall thought *Titanic* had been steaming west at 22.5. With that information, he calculated a position. We know he erred, because we found *Titanic* roughly 13.5 miles east-southeast of the position that Phillips radioed. The map, right, shows typical prevailing currents in April. The easterly Gulf Stream would have slowed *Titanic*'s progress west, explaining the 13.5-mile miscalculation. Before sinking, *Titanic* was also pushed south and west of the berg by a variation of the Labrador Stream, as evidenced by the location of the lifeboats *Carpathia* found, and by the wreckage. The stern probably sank straight down to its resting point at 41° 44' N, 49° 57' W. Survivors went to New York; one saved the bronze lifeboat burgee, above, now in the Titanic Historical Society museum.

The lifeboats' unexpected position makes sense in light of our discovery that *Titanic* sank southeast of its radioed CQD position. And that, in turn, reopens the issue of the location of other ships that night. Among them was *Californian*. It had stopped in the same ice field that

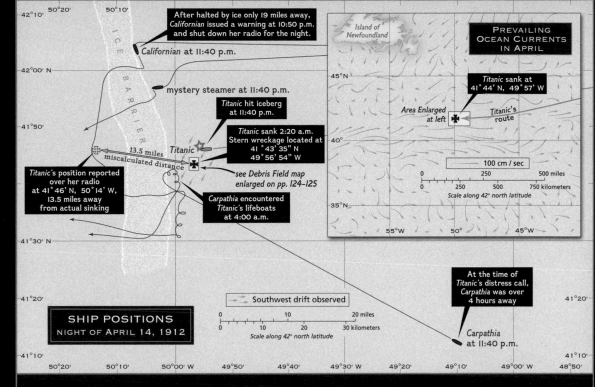

see Debris Field map enlarged on pp. 124-125

After halted by ice only 19 miles away, *Californian* **issued a warning at 10:50 p.m. and shut down her radio for the night.**

Californian at 11:40 p.m.

mystery steamer at 11:40 p.m.

Titanic hit iceberg at 11:40 p.m.

Titanic sank 2:20 a.m. Stern wreckage located at 41° 43' 35" N 49° 56' 54" W

Titanic's position reported over her radio at 41° 46' N, 50° 14' W, 13.5 miles away from actual sinking

13.5 miles miscalculated distance

Titanic

Carpathia encountered *Titanic's* lifeboats at 4:00 a.m.

At the time of *Titanic's* distress call, *Carpathia* was over 4 hours away

Carpathia at 11:40 p.m.

Southwest drift observed

SHIP POSITIONS
NIGHT OF APRIL 14, 1912

0   10   20 miles
0   10   20   30 kilometers
Scale along 42° north latitude

Island of Newfoundland

PREVAILING OCEAN CURRENTS IN APRIL

Titanic sank at 41° 44' N, 49° 57' W

Area Enlarged at left

Titanic's route

100 cm / sec

0   250   500 miles
0   250   500   750 kilometers
Scale along 42° north latitude

Titanic encountered and undoubtedly also began to drift. *Californian's* position, as figured by its captain, Stanley Lord, was about 19 miles north-northeast of *Titanic*.

At 11 p.m. on April 14, a *Californian* officer saw ship's lights in the southeast. The ship stopped at 11:40. Rockets began appearing after midnight and ended at 1:40 a.m., but Lord's ship did not respond. After 2 a.m., the unknown ship disappeared, seemingly by steaming to the southwest. British and American inquiries concluded *Californian* had seen *Titanic*. However, Lord maintained that *Californian* instead had witnessed a third vessel, usually dubbed the "mystery ship." Similarly, Lord argued that a vessel sighted by *Titanic* was that same mystery ship.

Titanic's true position lies southeast of *Californian's* calculated position, not southwest as had been previously believed. That would lend a bit of support to Lord's story. The ship his crew saw would not have appeared to steam southwest if it sank to the southeast. However, the same current that caused Boxhall to miscalculate *Titanic's* longitude may have affected *Californian* as well. It's possible *Californian* was east of where Lord said it was.

This map proposes one scenario. My own belief is that *Californian* was about 21 miles from *Titanic*, close enough to see rockets. The evidence suggests to me that the rockets *Californian's* officers witnessed came from *Titanic*—and that a rescue mission could have been launched.

Hillary and Tenzing Norgay standing in the thin air atop Everest. We drank it in for a few moments. At some point I exhaled. Then, unarguably out of time, Ralph dropped *Alvin*'s weights and started our ascent. He had kept us on the floor longer than advisable, given the leak. The malfunction was not life-threatening, but prolonged neglect could have ruined the submersible for subsequent dives. We had to get *Alvin* to the surface for repairs.

J. J.'s and *Alvin*'s handlers worked overnight to ensure that both would be ready for the second dive. On this descent, Martin Bowen replaced Dudley Foster. First we had to land *Alvin* on a safe spot. In the months leading up to the expedition, we had created a photomosaic of *Titanic* by piecing together 108 still pictures from *ANGUS*, which gave us a pretty good idea of conditions on the deck. We needed strong, flat places that could hold our submersible and provide access to the interior.

GHOSTLY *in the darkness,* Titanic's *prow suggests majesty even on the ocean floor in this image from* Alvin's *visit.*

Several spots looked scary. Cables draped the fallen foremast, which lay across the well deck and its inviting hatches. We'd have to avoid snagging *Alvin* in their clutches. Farther aft, the roof of the officers' quarters had fallen in. The best spot appeared to be a little farther back, next to the entrance to the forward Grand Staircase. The ornate glass dome once arching over it had vanished, allowing us access.

VIDEO IMAGES *of* Titanic's *interior were obtained by parking* Alvin *on the deck, then guiding* Jason Junior *down the stairwells— a tricky maneuver, performed beautifully.*

When we reached bottom, we encountered another series of snafus. *Alvin's* sonar was on the fritz, another short circuit compromised its electrical system, and flooding had knocked out *J. J.*'s motors. Another less-than-perfect trip, yet still our spirits soared as Ralph piloted *Alvin* in the first grand tour of *Titanic* in more than 74 years. We skirted then overflew the bow, struck by the truly "titanic" nature of everything aboard: anchor chains, capstans, steel plates. Rivulets of foamy, rusty slime dripped from the rails and other steel surfaces. *Alvin* touched one of the rusticles, which exploded into a muddy cloud. Scientists later discovered that these bacterial formations fed upon the ship's iron. Even after seven decades, they

had a long way to go before completing their work. Mollusks had attacked *Titanic*'s decks, and an army of one- to two-inch worms had consumed the woodwork.

Ralph landed *Alvin* briefly at two deck sites to test their strength, then headed for the Grand Staircase, where we verified that we could gain access to the interior. Then we swung along the side of the bow and peeked at A and B decks from the port side. It was easy to imagine men and women in Edwardian dress walking along the promenades or glancing back at us from the other side of the portholes.

Two hours and fifty minutes of exploration passed quickly. We reluctantly returned to the surface for another night's work.

The third dive was the charm. We put *Alvin* on the highest deck, next to the open shaft of the Grand Staircase. It was time for *J. J.* to shine. Martin coaxed the little blue 'bot out of its garage, then dropped it along the staircase's forward wall and down. One of the first images startled us with the undeniable fact of its own existence. An elaborate light fixture had somehow survived the ship's

tremendous impact with the sea floor. It remained attached to the ceiling although it had acquired a feathery sea pen as organic ornamentation. Its video image, captured by *J. J.*, became one of the expedition's most widely reproduced. It still bothers me that lack of time and recurring mechanical problems prevented us from getting a sharper still picture of the crystalline wonder.

Further dives would bring back an array of haunting images. The deck rail and anchor at *Titanic*'s bow. An open window in a first-class cabin. Buckling hull plates where an iceberg gash had been assumed. And a collection of winches, lights, a ceramic doll's head, a spittoon, a champagne bottle, the bronze steering telemotor, and a statue of Diana, goddess of the hunt, which may have been in the luggage of Denver millionaire Margaret "Molly" Brown.

Titanic's wood and iron generally had suffered the worst decay—the former eaten away and the latter covered by fans and stalactites of rusticles. Ceramic, glass, and bronze remained as bright as ever, especially where scoured by the current. Even some documents remained surprisingly intact. Clearly, some parts of the ship had fared better than others.

FRACTURED *by stress as the sea filled its forward compartments and pulled the stern out of the water,* Titanic *split into a bow section, foreground, a stern section, and debris that settled between and around the torn halves, as depicted in this painting.*

The expedition raised new questions about the environment at the bottom of the ocean, as well as what had happened on the night of April 14-15, 1912. It also demonstrated the potential for remotely operated vehicles, despite occasional malfunctions. When *J. J.* worked, it worked well, although it never got to perform the mission for which it was designed. The shadow in the images of *Scorpion* turned out to be flooring upturned by the sub's explosion, not an opening into its interior. But excitement generated by *J. J.*'s and *Alvin*'s visits to *Titanic* would help fund scientific deep-sea exploration and, we hoped, generate public opinion in favor of preserving *Titanic* and other shipwrecks.

Aside from pictures, we took nothing. We could have looted the debris field. The only time temptation threatened to get the better of me was when *Alvin* came upon a second-class purser's safe face-up in the mud, its bronze door handle beckoning. I ordered Alvin's claw to turn the handle, but the door remained fast. We let go and made pictures. When they were developed, they revealed that the safe's bottom had fallen away. The interior was empty.

NATURE'S OWN *ornament, a sea pen decorates a brass-and-crystal light fixture near the Grand Staircase. The dangling light originally hung from the ceiling.*

The ocean floor still remains one of the most inhospitable places in our biosphere. Water has nearly a thousand times the density of air, and the weight of some three miles of seawater overhead crushes almost anything with an air cavity—ship, submersible, or human body. Given such a hostile environment, *Titanic* seemed likely to enjoy a measure of peace in its final resting ground when I left it. As a further safeguard, the R.M.S. *Titanic* Maritime Memorial Act of 1986, signed by President Reagan, urged that *Titanic* be turned into an international memorial and left undisturbed. Congress said that pending an international agreement, it desired that "no person should physically alter, disturb, or salvage R.M.S. *Titanic.*"

But in international waters, American law has only the limited power of public opinion behind it. Despite the potential for negative press and the obstacles to visitation, including the cost of chartering the few submersibles capable of such depths, *Titanic* is literally in danger of being loved to death.

Here is where the media can become friends. *Titanic* creates an audience that larger social issues cannot draw on their own. The future of undersea exploration is being decided, now. How should the more than a million shipwrecks in the Atlantic, Pacific, Mediterranean and other international bodies of water be governed? Who decides whether they will be salvaged or explored peacefully in situ? Pillaged or protected? And what is the best way to glimpse their frozen moments of history? Most voters and legislators yawn at such questions, but they sit up and pay attention when they see *Titanic*.

In the years since *Titanic*'s discovery, further expeditions and James Cameron's 1997 movie, the highest-grossing motion picture of all time, have increased the attention on the ship. Proposed laws governing shipwrecks, including *Titanic* specifically, have been dusted off and given new readings. Congress originally ordered U.S. talks with Britain, France, and Canada about preserving *Titanic*. The four nations hammered out a draft agreement in 2000 but stalled until December 2003, when the British government became the first to sign the international agreement to protect the shipwreck as a memorial to all who died when it sank. The agreement bans unapproved dives as inconsistent

AT HOME *in* Titanic's *graveyard, a rat-tail fish examines a chamber pot and bottles in the debris field.*

with the ship's status as a grave and artifact. Visitors would need permission from the governments signing the agreement. As of this writing, two of the four nations have signed it into a treaty—the U. S. and Great Britain. *Titanic* has become a test case for future underwater preserves, an oceanic version of Antarctica, which remains a pristine place for scientific study thanks to its status as an international park.

Until Congress enacts the treaty, the U.S. has only a set of National Oceanic and Atmospheric Administration (NOAA) guidelines for *Titanic* research, exploration, and salvage. Published in the *Federal Register*, they discourage any activities that would accelerate deterioration, including cutting holes in the hull, and allow visits only in the name of "educational, scientific, or cultural interests." Recovery of artifacts "in the public interest" may occur, but NOAA emphatically said, "The preferred policy for the preservation of R.M.S. *Titanic* and its artifacts is in-situ preservation."

Titanic sits on the ocean floor as the pyramids sat atop the Egyptian desert or classical temples sat atop the hills of Greece. At one time, such historical sites were filled with pottery, artwork, stonework, and other artifacts. French, British, and German archaeologists and art lovers plundered these ancient treasures and packed their booty off to museums. Thousands of valuable artifacts have been removed from context and put on display far away. At the time of their removal, relocation seemed to make sense, but now we have

airports, jets, and hotels. Tourists flock to the Nile by the millions. Imagine visiting *Titanic* and finding it much as it was in 1912. It would be like visiting a mountain range instead of holding a rock.

The analogy comparing *Titanic* to the pyramids is particularly apt when you recall that both are tombs. The ship's debris field once contained hundreds of bodies that scattered as the broken hull sank. Natural processes have taken their flesh and bones and left only bits of clothing and other personal items. One of *ANGUS*'s most poignant photographs depicts a pair of boots on the ocean floor. Heels point in, toes out, as if the owner wore them in death. Shoes on the ocean floor give mute testimony to the sacredness of the site.

Inside *Titanic*'s hull sections, bodies of trapped passengers and crewmen surely remain. By what right can anyone treat the graveyard of *Titanic*, which still resides in the living memory of its passengers at the time of this writing, like the tombs of the ancient world? Would it not be like taking belt buckles or wristwatches off the U.S.S. *Arizona*, or personal effects from the site of the World Trade Center?

After returning from *Knorr*'s voyage in 1985, I told Congress that the intact sections of *Titanic* should remain undisturbed. I also gave my opinion that artifacts from the debris field should be recovered and put on display to ensure their protection and availability to the eyes of the world. Those who favor salvaging items often use that statement to support their position. I wish I could take it back. I gave my testimony before having the opportunity to discuss the future of *Titanic* in depth with museum curators, historians, and scientists. For a variety of reasons, they agree there is little purpose in removing *Titanic* items from the ocean floor. Most of the personal items are Edwardian bric-a-brac of no real archaeological value, and the ship's items

ACTOR *Leonardo DiCaprio, who played fictional passenger Jack Dawson in James Cameron's film* Titanic, *signs an autograph at the 1997 London premiere.*

bulkheads have shielded its insides from the worst ravages of time. As interior explorations have revealed, the farther one goes inside *Titanic*, the better the preservation.

Thanks to twists of maritime law, American courts ruled that my team did not "officially" discover *Titanic* because we did not bring back any part of the ship. The first to take things from a wreck in international waters can claim exclusive

are not unique. The few goods of intrinsic value would cost more to recover than they are worth. Furthermore, survivors compare the removal of artifacts to grave robbing.

And finally, despite arguments from salvagers, there is little worry about deterioration of remaining artifacts. I suspect that *Titanic*'s deterioration curve is asymptotic, most of the damage done in the first few years after its sinking, and after that, a long, slow, natural process. Beautifully intact are thousands of porcelain and glass objects, as well as leather treated with tannic acid. Thousands of years of exposure to the open ocean will not dissolve *Titanic*'s dishes and drinking glasses, terra cotta or porcelain. *Titanic*'s

rights to come back and take more. We could have done so when *ANGUS* accidentally snared a piece of *Titanic* cable which, sold to collectors, would have brought a fortune. But fortune hunting was not why we visited. Unwilling to take any part of the ship, we threw the cable overboard. If I found *Titanic* today, I could have filed for exclusive visitation rights and gained a measure of control.

Since then the ship seemingly has worn an "open season" sign. Submersibles repeatedly have

A FIRST-CLASS *dinner plate, following pages, left, brought to the surface from* Titanic *by salvagers, shows no sign of wear. At right, the White Star logo remains sharp and clear on a salvaged silver artifact.*

A PURSER'S *bag retrieved from* Titanic *contained coins, keys, watches, jewelry, and other items.*

visited. Some have landed on its decks, assaulting the already stressed deck plates and possibly accelerating the spread of gaping holes. Some have removed objects from the debris field and the ship itself. Through it all, *Titanic* has suffered.

"The danger lies not in man's greed but in his curiosity," *Titanic* historian Walter Lord wrote in 1986. He was right. The ship needs a protocol not only for preservation, but also for exploration. When you go into a room in Thomas Jefferson's Monticello, the staff doesn't let you sit on the furniture. We need a law to govern those who would visit the Monticellos of the deep.

WHEN WE LEFT TITANIC in 1986, we purposefully did not publicize its exact location in order to discourage a stampede of visitors. However, our French colleagues knew. Still stung by the unintended media frenzy that had left them in the cold in 1985, IFREMER sought to finance its own return to *Titanic*.

It already had the technology: *Nautile*, a titanium submersible nearly nine feet wide, weighing 19½ tons, and capable of diving to 20,000 feet. Its foot-thick plastic windows permitted a crew of pilot, copilot, and observer to scan the ocean floor and observe through real-time video images their operation of mechanical arms that could pick up artifacts to be carried to the surface. The object of *Nautile*'s expeditions was more than observation.

The French government had helped pay for the development of *Nautile* and indirectly subsidized its rental to fortune seekers. For more financial backing, the team latched onto a Connecticut car salesman who had European connections through his running the largest BMW dealership in the United States. He aimed to turn a profit on his investments in the dives by taking possession of recovered *Titanic* artifacts. Over the next few years, his Titanic Ventures team, which evolved into a company called RMS Titanic Inc., sank many millions of dollars into a series of salvage operations. RMS Titanic Inc. likened the collection of artifacts to the restoration of Colonial Williamsburg. To me, the salvage job seemed more like plowing the fields of Gettysburg.

Nautile's 32 dives in the summer of 1987 grabbed about 1,800 objects from the debris field and the ship itself. These included luggage, a compass, a leather bag, brass uniform buttons bearing the White Star emblem, a sapphire and diamond ring, a bronze cherub statue from the Grand Staircase, and half of baggage receipt No. 208. (The other half remained with passenger Lawrence Beesley as he made his way to safety.) The recovery of such objects resulted in the team's establishing a claim to be sole "salvors in possession." The

law is a glorified version of "finders, keepers."

Since visits began by Titanic Ventures and subsequent salvagers, many more objects have disappeared. Gone is a bell from the foremast where lookout Frederick Fleet first spotted the fatal iceberg. Gone, too, is a mast light, firmly attached when I saw it in 1986. Salvagers claim that it was fragile and they didn't want it to fall and break on the deck.

Sadly, the crow's nest we saw in 1986 also was ruined, perhaps in salvagers' eagerness to retrieve the ship's telephone inside. They hold that they recovered the phone from the debris field. On our return in 2004 we did notice that a block we saw dangling from a davit had disappeared, as had a drape of rigging over the forecastle. Much of it appeared to have been cut away, perhaps, we hypothesized, to provide *Nautile* access to the bow so it could shine up *Titanic*'s name for the cameras.

I made my objections known but could not match the tenor of expressions of indignation that came from shipwreck survivor Eva Hart. As a young girl, she had played with her teddy bear on *Titanic*'s sunny decks. On the night of April 14-15, 1912, her father insisted she get into a lifeboat while he stayed behind. She watched the stern carry him to his death. Seventy-five years later a retired welfare officer and justice of the peace near London, she assaulted the 1987 expedition in no uncertain terms: "To bring up those things from a mass sea grave just to make a few thousand pounds shows a dreadful insensitivity and greed.

The grave should be left alone. They're simply going to do it as fortune hunters, vultures, pirates!"

Connecticut Senator Lowell Weicker reacted to the *Nautile* venture by sponsoring a bill to prohibit the sale or display for profit of salvaged *Titanic* artifacts in the United States. That touched off a debate that still rages today.

On one side are those who agree with columnist William F. Buckley, whom the French invited to visit *Titanic* in 1987. He weighed in publicly in the *New York Times* magazine, saying, "You hardly consecrate the artifacts that went down on the *Titanic* by leaving them on the ocean floor." He equated arguments that the salvagers exploited *Titanic* with specious arguments that Paul Gauguin exploited Tahiti—as if Gauguin had removed much of Tahiti to France! On the other side of the debate, Wilbur Garrett, then editor of NATIONAL GEOGRAPHIC, stated that the French expedition to retrieve artifacts had been justifiably condemned as grave robbing, "for the line between curiosity and acquisitiveness seems to have been crossed."

If the public has a hard time distinguishing between true archaeologists and pirates, we might blame Hollywood. Careful, rigorous archaeological inquiry requires many hours of thinking, planning, and analyzing for every hour in the field. Recovered objects must be lovingly preserved and appropriately displayed. Many people would find the work boring.

Compare that with the popular image of the archaeologist: Indiana Jones, cracking his whip, grabbing a golden statue or a holy relic, and hightailing it to a waiting plane or submarine a few seconds ahead of the bad guys. The problem is, Indiana Jones is not acting as a true archaeologist when he takes his treasures back to his college office. As dashing as he is, he's a pirate. But that's a hard idea to sell.

The 1987 expedition spent more than six times as many hours as *Alvin* did on the ocean floor, most of it in recovering artifacts. The salvagers began restoring the objects but have done little to guarantee their perpetual preservation. Archaeologists are extremely selective in what they take from a historical site because of the tremendous burden of care. I remove objects only at the express request of scientific experts, and then only when they demonstrate the need for specific items as a path for legitimate inquiry.

On one recent expedition, for example, my team found nearly 800 well-preserved amphorae on the floor of the Mediterranean Sea, resting where a Phoenician shipwreck deposited them 2,700 years ago. We brought up *nine*. The scientists interested in understanding the culture that made these giant jars said they needed that many to study the precision of manufacturing techniques. Once we determined that the amphorae had been made to incredibly exacting standards, with literally millimeters of difference from one jar to the

AMPHORAE *from a Roman shipwreck were taken on my 2003 Mediterranean expedition for scientific study only.*

next, we rejected the need to retrieve any more. It would serve no scientific purpose. Nor would the amphorae bring any income. Selling such ancient cultural artifacts is illegal.

When we do remove an object from the ocean, we carefully document where we found it. Site mapping helps scientists understand more about cultures, ships, and shipwrecks. Salvage expeditions did little to treat *Titanic* as an archaeological site and document the location of each artifact. Small exhibitions in Paris, Olso, and other European cities displayed the recovered and refurbished objects, most often requiring viewers to pay an admission fee. A second French expedition in 1993, backed in part by a stock offering, recovered more artifacts and spurred more museum exhibitions. Thousands of people lined up to see such ordinary objects as a pair of eyeglasses and a silver coffee service brought up from the underwater burial ground of the *Titanic*. During 1994 and 1995, nearly three-quarters of a million people trooped through the National Maritime Museum in Greenwich, England, to view its largest display to date.

The scientific and academic community had a far different response, roundly condemning the

Greenwich museum for its tacit endorsement of the salvagers' actions. Amid a series of similar maritime recovery projects made possible by the emerging deep-sea technology, the Council of American Maritime Museums inserted a rule in its bylaws prohibiting the display of maritime objects recovered without scientific oversight.

The salvagers returned in French and Russian submersibles to *Titanic* in 1994, 1996, 1998, and 2000. Dozens of dives brought the number of recovered artifacts to 6,000, with the first reaching American soil in 1993. Salvaged objects ranged from the inconsequential to the gigantic. Early dives brought to the surface hundreds of pieces of coal from Titanic's Boiler Room No. 1. Although the salvagers had promised not to sell *Titanic* artifacts for profit to individual collectors, they began advertising "Authentic Anthracite From The 1912 Maiden Voyage" at $25 a lump. (Museum gift shops today charge $20 for a bit of *Titanic* coal the size of a pinkie fingernail.) Sales helped finance the ambitious 1996 expedition. That voyage had Bass Ale, supplier to the White Star Line, on board as a financial sponsor. In return for a large check

THE ROBOTIC *arm of a salvager's submersible reaches for a leaded glass window in* Titanic's *debris field.*

and some valuable publicity, the expedition retrieved a handful of Bass bottles from the debris field.

For sheer spectacle, nothing could compare with the 1996 effort to salvage what came to be known as the "Big Piece." Newspaper stories and advertising stirred up interest in plans for recovering a loose chunk of the hull measuring 20 by 24 feet, and invited the curious to spend anywhere from $500 to more than $10,000 to cruise to the site and watch the salvage efforts.

The quarry—the 18-ton Big Piece, identified as coming from C deck, cabins C-79 and C-81, on the starboard side—lay by itself in the mud. *Nautile* attached four 5,000-gallon bags of diesel fuel to the Big Piece. The lighter-than-water fuel then lifted it to within 200 feet of the surface. RMS Titanic Inc. planned to drag the piece underwater toward the American coast so that it could dramatically enter New York Harbor, symbolically ending the interrupted journey from Southhampton.

Hurricane Eduardo had other ideas. The storm moved up the eastern seaboard and churned up the surface waters of the Atlantic. Stresses and strains multiplied on the cables until they finally parted, and the Big Piece dropped to the bottom of the ocean once again. Those who had opposed the salvage operation may have discerned some divine comment in the disaster. The salvagers returned in 1998, however, and finally brought up the Big Piece. They put it on display in Tampa, Florida.

Despite such efforts, no recovery team has brought up a truly important historical artifact from the wreck of the *Titanic*. There has been nothing like the log of Captain E. J. Smith, for instance, or film from passengers' cameras that might shed light on the tragic events of 1912.

Despite the public's fascination with all things *Titanic*, RMS Titanic Inc. suffered a precipitous drop in its stock price and found it difficult to turn a profit by selling exhibition tickets. It asked a federal judge for the rights to sell recovered artifacts but was turned down. After a shareholder lawsuit and other headaches, the RMS Titanic corporation announced in September 2002 that it planned to surrender its rights of salvage at some unspecified date and make no further trips to the shipwreck.

Alas, that did not stop rumors of an unidentified and illegal team of salvagers visiting *Titanic*. A satellite photo implied a surface ship at the site in the fall of 2002, and an investigator's report to a federal court in Norfolk, Virginia, hinted that a private French company's submarine had made the dive late that year.

"Salvage may have taken place in the bow of the wreck using a remotely operated vehicle," the investigator reported. The pilot of the submersible told the *New York Times* that the pirates caused a lot of damage in trying to recover the pedestal of the bridge wheel, the only thing still standing in the middle of the bridge.

The two main camps that argue about *Titanic*'s future seem to divide between the "Rest in Peace" and the "Wrest a Piece" contingents. And there is a third group. Documentary and feature filmmakers have visited the wreck to light the darkness and capture its magic for paying theatergoers. The Russians hire out their submersibles, *Mir I* and *Mir II*, to those who want to explore *Titanic*. A Russian-Canadian-American team spent 140 hours

on the ocean floor in 1991 and exposed more than 40,000 feet of IMAX film to create their documentary, *Titanica*. The Russians returned in 1995 with Hollywood director James Cameron. The cost of gathering authentic images of *Titanic* to intercut with his fictional portrayal of its maiden voyage helps explain his movie's price tag of $200 million.

The unseen costs may have included damage to *Titanic*. Rumors floated that during the filming the Russians suffered a scary but non-fatal accident. A French submersible later found a two-foot piece of fiberglass in an officer's room, perhaps fallen from

THE "BIG PIECE," *a section of* Titanic's *hull, rests on the deck of the French recovery ship* Abeille.

the damaged *Mir*. They also found that the wooden frame of the skylight above the Marconi room had been pulled free, and more *Mir* debris reportedly was found there.

Cameron has become one of the most frequent visitors to *Titanic*. He returned to the ship in 2001 for a series of dives to get high-definition photographs for a book and three-dimensional movie. He brought along two ROVs developed by his brother, Mike, and a custom-designed lighting system to illuminate the ship for his cameras.

Jake and *Elwood*, his tethered robots, had been designed to fit into small openings in the hull. Their agility allowed them to penetrate much farther into the interior than previous expeditions had been able to do. What they found was both awe-inspiring and depressing as new details came to light. Five-foot-high leaded-glass windows were surprisingly intact, their patterns still clear, on D deck. Although pine walls had nearly vanished, carved mahogany paneling remained in place, four decks from the top—evidence that dense forms of wood, at least, survived the ravages of time better

THE RUSSIAN *submersible* Mir II *hovers over* Titanic's *forecastle. James Cameron used it and its twin,* Mir I, *to film the shipwreck.*

when sealed off from the open ocean. Thick walls also protected the "Silent Room," the soundproofed space containing the heavy, noisy machinery that generated the spark for transmitting the messages that the Marconi operators sent by clicking the radio key next door.

The state of preservation is so high there that it's possible to verify how Harold Bride set the field regulator handles as he tried to wring more power for Phillips' desperate calls for assistance. The open switch on the direct current panel indicates Phillips deliberately cut the power before finally leaving his post. However, artist Ken Marschall wrote after visiting the radio site during the Cameron expedition, "No definitive examination of the Marconi antenna roof connection is now possible because so much sub activity has pretty much scoured and scraped the area, a popular landing spot over the years. . . . I saw no landmarks, no sign of the fittings and vent that were there when the wreck was first photographed by *ANGUS*."

When Cameron's robots worked their way into the ship's staterooms, they made more discoveries.

A wash cabinet, upright and intact, held an upright drinking carafe and glass in their specially designed holders, suggesting that the cabin's occupant poured a drink on the ship's last day.

A few items of clothing have survived as well, especially those in contact with metal objects or wires, which emit small electrical currents that discourage microbial activity. Stateroom D-33 contained a fashionable bowler hat, resting on its side amid tumbled, rust-colored debris. The room had been occupied by 47-year-old Henry Harper, whose grandfather had helped create the publishing house of Harper and Brothers. Harper survived the sinking, as did his wife, servant, and Pekingese dog. In a memoir for his family-run *Harper's Weekly*, he recalled watching the fatal iceberg pass by his cabin's porthole. Perhaps in his haste to get to Lifeboat No. 3, Harper left his hat.

Cameron also found great deterioration since the ship's discovery in 1985. Ken Marschall studied photographs from the 1985 and '86 expeditions to create stunning paintings of the ship for books and magazines, and he knew what had changed in a decade and a half. The deck had fallen in the stern section. The collapse had brought the portholes of C deck within a few feet of the boat deck. Holes had expanded in the decks of the bow section. The walls of officers' quarters had fallen in, as had the railings at the bridge. Captain Smith's bathroom had lost all claim to privacy after the collapse of its outer wall. In 1986, the roof above the Reading and Writing Room had been true and level, except for a two-foot hole. Marschall's 2001 visit found the entire roof collapsed at the forward end.

We also know that since my initial visit, the port bow gangway door, which Second Officer Charles Herbert Lightoller opened as the ship sank, has disappeared. A huge section of promenade deck has vanished, too. The gymnasium, where an exercise instructor suggested that passengers stay warm on the "mechanical camels" as they awaited a seat in the lifeboats, has lost its roof. The whole gym now tilts, its starboard wall a mess.

Visitors have left things as well as taken them. Many visitors to the bridge have deposited plaques and other memorials at the edge of the wheelhouse's teak foundation. Artificial flowers, plastic sampling bags, a fishing net, lead weights, and even beer and soda bottles (apparently tossed overboard from passing ships) litter the decks. One special memorial has disappeared. Marschall reported that the plaque we left on the stern in 1986 is now missing. "It has either slid off from its precarious position on the edge of the fairlead or been intentionally removed," he wrote.

And the most recent visitors noted changes that have happened even in the last couple of years. "I was shocked," said Alfred McLaren, a scientist who dived to *Titanic* in 1999 and 2003. "It's much more heavily deteriorated," says McLaren. "I expected to see her in about the same shape. . . . But

MIR I AND MIR II *illuminate the leaning bulkhead of the captain's cabin from front and rear.*

God Almighty, there's more [rust] everywhere." A submersible pilot who has visited more than 30 times agrees, saying that every dive reveals more damage.

How much this deterioration results from natural decay and how much from the repeated landing and maneuvering of submersibles is a matter for scientific inquiry. Rusticles do seem thicker now. Some biologists have suggested that the bacteria consuming the ship's iron have accelerated the rate of decay. They cite the likelihood of microbes increasing their surface area for digestion by exploiting cracks and crannies, much the

same way tooth decay speeds up when it gets a foothold in a cavity. Perhaps the rate of microbial decay is linked to human disturbances, however. Examining the literature since my last visit, I suspect that it is visitors who have done the greatest damage.

"When the ship went down, it would have seemed unimaginable that someday visitors to the watery grave of that grand liner would be numerous enough to threaten its survival," the *New York Times* editorialized in 2003.

"But then the ship's going down in the first place seemed unimaginable, too." ■

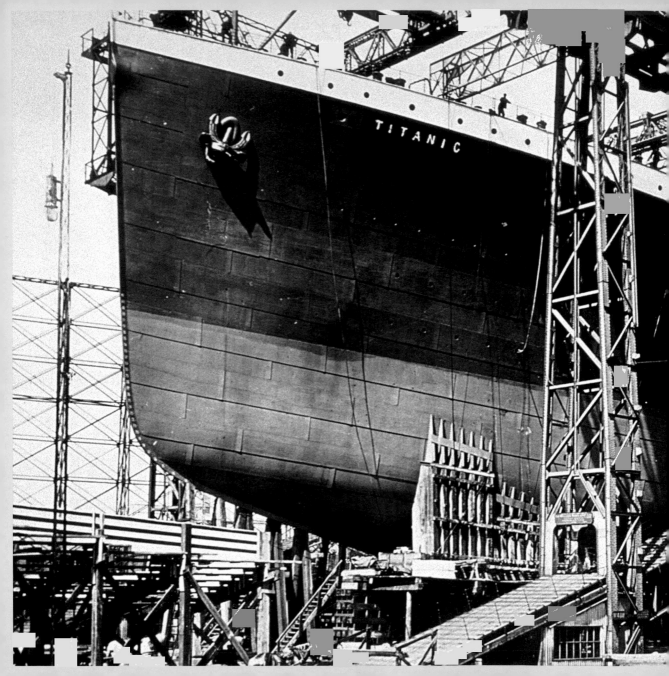

THE BOW

For all its bulk, Titanic never lacked grace. Belfast shipbuilders Harland & Wolff took inspiration from yachts' shapes and merged gently curving hull lines with a well-proportioned superstructure. Nowhere was devotion to beauty more obvious than in the lines of the bow, left, here protruding from the stocks as the ship neared its launch date. Even after 92 years on the ocean floor, the bow retains an athletic elegance, above, despite underwater intruders. No wonder James Cameron set a vivid scene of his film right here.

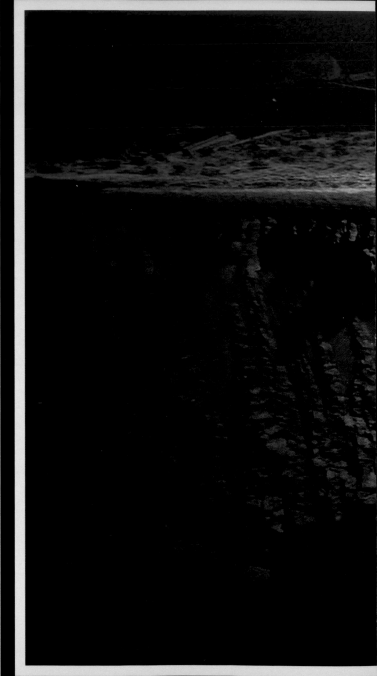

FRAMED ENTIRELY *of steel and measuring 175 feet from keel to funnel top,* Titanic *dominated the Harland & Wolff shipyard, above, two months before its maiden voyage. Shipbuilders fashioned the bow to take a pounding as* Titanic *surged through the North Atlantic at more than 20 knots.*

THE BOW SECTION *sank intact after* Titanic *broke apart between the third and fourth funnels. Much of it is still in good shape. A round deck light and port window, right, near the No. 1 funnel appear nearly functional even today.*

CHAPTER THREE

TOOLS *for* EXPLORATION

THE TOWED SLED ANGUS, *equipped with still-frame cameras, heads for Titanic in 1985.*

MAKING PREDICTIONS can be risky. A little more than two decades ago, I took a crack at it. In retrospect, my vision probably ranks as one of the most audacious in the history of oceanography. But since it was based on hard science, I felt confident.

My dream was to use "telepresence" to explore the ocean floor. Sensitive cameras in remotely controlled vehicles would capture images from the deep and send them to a ship far above. Circuits on board the ship would uplink the information to a communications satellite 22,000 miles overhead. The satellite would share the data with distant observers, so that anyone, virtually anywhere, could explore the ocean depths in real time.

I had been fine-tuning my vision of the future for two years in 1981, when I took a fateful walk down the hallway at the National Geographic Society building in Washington, D.C. A senior assistant editor, Samuel W. Matthews, collared me and said he was preparing an issue of the magazine on the world's oceans. "I want you to sit down with the art department and create a vision of the future of exploration," he said.

So I shared my vision of telepresence. "A pilot-scientist aboard the surface ship will sit before a bank of TV screens," I told Matthews. "Far below him, 'flying' at the end of a cable some hundred feet above the bottom, an unmanned exploring craft will carry supersensitive imaging cameras and lights, capable of recording as much as four acres of

THE WOODS HOLE *Oceanographic Institution in Massachusetts served as home base for the first expeditions to* Titanic *aboard the research vessels* Atlantis II, *then* Knorr.

seafloor at once." The towed exploration vehicle would have a forward-looking sonar to watch for what lay in its path and side-scanning sonar to examine the contours of the ocean floor. When the vehicle's real-time video captured an intriguing image, operators aboard the mother ship would dispatch a smaller, more maneuverable vehicle to investigate. The small vehicle would gather specimens with a robotic arm or record close-up images with its own high-resolution cameras. All of the data would go up the communications chain to the satellite—and the world.

Aside from the orbiting communications satellite, none of this vision existed at the time. But by the beginning of the new century, the vision was complete. I had stumbled upon other aspects of the necessary technology in 1979 while working on plate-tectonics research during a sabbatical at Stanford University. Mountains of color slides from a series of deep-sea expeditions filled my study in Palo Alto, yet I had explored and recorded less than 50 miles of the 40,000-mile Mid-Ocean Ridge beneath our planet's watery skin. My frustration lay with the only options available at the time for deep-sea exploration: towed camera sleds, such as *ANGUS,* and manned submersibles.

Towed sleds covered a lot more territory than submersibles but were blind. They had to be hauled to the surface, their photo negatives developed and printed, then examined by a scientist, before the decision could be made to explore further.

Meanwhile the ship towing the photo sled might be long gone or hard-pressed to double back.

Manned submersibles, the other option, were handicapped by limited mobility as well as the risks inherent in sending air-breathing humans into deep waters.

Humans had been exploring the deep only since June 11, 1930, when two Americans, Charles William Beebe and Otis Barton, had themselves sealed into a steel ball and lowered by cable 1,426 feet into the water near the island of Bermuda. Combining its shape with the Greek word for "deep," Beebe christened his craft a "bathysphere."

The technology was crude. Divers entered the sphere, less than five feet tall, through a 15-inch hole. There was barely enough room for them, along with their oxygen tanks, to fit in. A support crew screwed the 400-pound door shut and tightened it with ten giant bolts and an eight-inch wing nut that had to be hammered into position. Three fused-quartz windows, eight inches across and three inches thick, let the occupants peer out. Despite all shortcomings, Beebe and Barton dropped three times farther into the watery depths than any other human and lived to tell about it. Their bathysphere descents ultimately took them more than half a mile down.

Still, survival remained an issue. As deep-sea submersibles improved, they continued to require flawless design and construction if their occupants expected to return alive to the realm of air and light.

Human error being what it is, death always looked over the shoulder of any deep-sea adventurer. Submarine disasters, including the fatal explosion in 2000 aboard the *Kursk*, finest of Russia's Oscar II-class subs, remind us that we haven't eradicated this problem.

In 1947, Swiss physicist Auguste Piccard—whose students included pioneering French oceanographer Jacques Cousteau—merged an improved version of Beebe and Barton's pressure sphere with a flotation tank. Piccard's bathyscaph ("deep boat") acted like a balloon, falling and climbing by becoming heavier or lighter than surrounding water. In the early 1950s Piccard created *Trieste,* a pressure sphere more than seven feet across with a skin of hard, forged-steel alloy and a 50-foot flotation tank filled with 22,000 gallons of gasoline. With *Trieste,* a cable connection to a surface ship was no longer needed. Divers descended by flooding two air tanks and replacing some gasoline in the overhead reservoir with seawater. The bathyscaph became heavier than the surrounding fluid and started to sink. To ascend, the sphere's occupants magnetically dropped a load of iron pellets and gained buoyancy.

In 1960 Jacques Piccard and an American naval officer, Lt. Don Walsh, piloted *Trieste* to the bottom of Challenger Deep, deepest point in the western Pacific's Marianas Trench—at 35,800 feet down, the lowest place on the planet, more than a mile deeper than Mount Everest is tall. The pressure

A PROPHETIC DRAWING *which appeared in the December 1981 issue of* NATIONAL GEOGRAPHIC *shares my vision of deep-sea exploration. Green indicates coverage by Argo's video cameras. Pink represents sonar. Jason, at bottom at the end of a tether, explores the ocean bed.*

ALVIN'S CRAMPED INTERIOR, *following pages, left, is my home for a 1977 descent to the Galapagos Rift. William Beebe, right, emerging from the bathysphere in 1930, had it even tighter.*

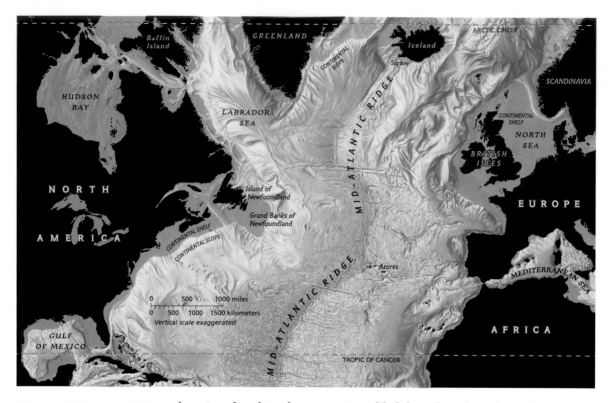

MID-ATLANTIC RIDGE, *where I explored in* Alvin *in 1974, yielded data about how the seafloor forms.*

of Challenger Deep measures 16,000 pounds per square inch. One of *Trieste*'s windows cracked under the strain, but it surfaced intact. Walsh and Piccard had succeeded. Their dive proved that *Trieste* could withstand great depths. No human has ever made a follow-up trip to Challenger Deep.

Trieste's singular triumph confirmed for me that the ocean would someday be as accessible as any mountaintop or desert. I imagined scientists living on the surface and setting up outposts beneath the waves, even on the seafloor. Still, bathyscaphs

and bathyspheres were not the solution. Their size and weight made them unwieldy. They moved like sophisticated yo-yos, up and down but not horizontally. The next generation of manned submersibles, such as *Alvin,* had thrusters that let them move about, but at less than a walking pace. Their underwater stays were still limited by the crews' oxygen supplies. I wanted a system that could remain below indefinitely and provide real-time images like those seen by human eyes through a submersible's viewports.

In a fortunate bit of serendipity, living in Palo Alto I was in just the right spot to learn about coming technologies that could realize my vision. The nearby Silicon Valley computer industry was creating microchips, low-light video technology, and fiber-optic cables capable of high-speed data transmission. I began to envision a pair of unmanned exploration vehicles on the ocean floor, communicating in real time with the surface. One night before I fell asleep, I was reading Greek mythology. In the morning, I knew I would call my undersea explorers *Jason* and *Argo,* for the questing hero and the ship that carried him to distant lands

Our 2004 trip to the North Atlantic to visit *Titanic* embodied all aspects of that 1979 vision, shared with the world in a drawing published two years later in NATIONAL GEOGRAPHIC.

THE SURFACE SHIP was the *Ronald H. Brown,* a NOAA research vessel named for President Clinton's secretary of commerce, who died in a plane crash in Bosnia. This 274-foot, 3,250-ton ship, commissioned in 1997, has thousands of feet of lab space, including separate biology and electronics/computer labs. Its equipment includes a simple echo sounder, which finds the ocean floor, and a multi-beam echo sounder—a full-mounted sonar, which produces a three-dimensional image of the floor and is used in mapping. The

Ron Brown's stern and bow thrusters, linked to a global positioning signal, can park the ship within a meter of a given location on the ocean surface.

The stern is fitted with an A-frame and assorted cranes and winches for launching and retrieving smaller vehicles. Those designed to visit *Titanic* in 2004 were *Argus* and *Hercules,* well advanced beyond my 1979 vision. Both were designed by my chief engineer, Jim Newman, after I decided that the Institute for Exploration needed to create and operate its own exploration vehicles instead of competing for time on *Jason.* Jim is one of the key people who bought into the vision and helped make it a reality. He built *Argus* and *Hercules* to withstand the pressure at some 12,000 feet down and to maneuver effortlessly in response to commands from the surface.

Hercules a mobile, versatile ROV—carries thrusters, lights, and cameras, including a high-definition video system that can take stunningly detailed pictures. Strapped to the deck of the *Ron Brown,* it looks awkward: a rectangular frame seven feet tall, stuffed with electronics and topped with a bright yellow syntactic foam buoyancy package that resembles the lid of a giant beer cooler. In air, *Hercules* weighs nearly 5,000 pounds. Underwater, it can hover and fly weightlessly.

Herc was designed for archaeological excavations on the ocean floor, but needless to say, it would not be disturbing *Titanic.* Not only were we not interested in retrieving artifacts, we had been directed by NOAA to follow a "look but don't touch" exploration protocol. We had permission for *Hercules* to use its robotic arm to retrieve rusticle experiments left during previous expeditions and to place two new scientific platforms next to the ship. Other than that, *Hercules* would keep a reverential distance.

We had hoped to use a second ROV, the 500-pound *Little Hercules,* to look inside *Titanic*, but two weeks before the sailing date, NOAA informed my team that it would not allow any interior exploration—to minimize the risk of damage to the ship and respect the salvors' rights, we were told. Naturally we were disappointed not to visit the Grand Staircase and the many palatial rooms. We still took *Little Herc* along for the voyage, to pinch-hit if *Big Herc* suffered mechanical problems.

At the end of *Hercules's* tether was the towed sled *Argus*, the successor to *Argo,* which we used to photograph *Titanic* in 1985. Named for the builder of the mythological Jason's ship, *Argus* still must be connected by cable to a surface ship. An A-frame on the *Ron Brown* picks it up and lowers it over the stern. Its cable unspools as it descends. Operators watch *Argus's* progress on a video monitor from the main deck and send signals to adjust the maneuvers of the sled and its cameras.

Swimming silently and gracefully in three-dimensional space, *Hercules* comes close to embodying legendary Jacques Cousteau's ideal mode of deep-sea transportation: one that allows an explorer to move "like an angel." The key lies in not stretching the tether between *Herc* and *Argus*. The cable connecting *Argus* to the surface ship transmits every up or down motion as the ship rises or falls with the waves. These sudden jolts jerk *Argus's* frame but don't get transmitted to the ROV as long as the tether remains slack. The pilots have to keep their vehicles close to each other.

For the short, intense return to *Titanic,* we knew we'd do the best job possible with our new vehicles. *Argus* and both ROVs can still be used if some of their systems fail. You don't junk a car when the air conditioner gives out. Typically, a mission to the ocean floor starts with safe and simple tasks and gets riskier as time goes on. You want to collect plenty of data before you put your technology at risk, so you warm up, sort of like a sports event. As head of the mission, it's my job to figure out the best timetable and method for getting every desired photograph and piece of data.

When this system works, it exceeds the vision I described more than 20 years ago. Then, I wrote that the ROV system would extend a scientist's eyes and hands as he sat in the surface ship or in his land laboratory and watched the video feed—a point-to-point communication with one video channel. Instead, what my team envisioned for the return to *Titanic* was a live, multichannel broadcast to the public.

Communications signals were to be sent from the ship via satellite to a mobile satellite communications center that transmits the data to a hub in Plano,

Texas. The signals are turned into digital video, then transmitted to Internet2, a consortium of 205 universities, government agencies, and private industries working to create an advanced version of the Internet capable of delivering huge amounts of data. A key Internet2 receiving site is to be the new Inner Space Center at the University of Rhode Island's Graduate School of Oceanography, eventually slated to act for ocean exploration as the Johnson Space Center does for space missions. Engineers, archaeologists, geologists, and other experts will share information in real time with explorers at sea. At other U.S. sites, thousands more will participate in cutting-edge science through telepresence.

Realizing this vision of telepresence required two vital steps. First, private and public organizations such as the Office of Naval Research (ONR), the National Geographic Society, and NOAA had to support the idea. When the GEOGRAPHIC published its series of ocean exploration articles in December 1981, Matthews proclaimed that *Argo* and *Jason* were already being designed. That was

DANGLING *above a British barge, the Beebe-Barton bathysphere prepares for a dive near Bermuda.*

LEGEND RECORDS *Alexander the Great, depicted at top in a French manuscript, as the first to investigate the deep. Three centuries ago, scientist Edmund Halley used a bell similar to the one shown for experimental diving.*

stretching things a bit, but it attracted attention and money from ONR and helped development get under way.

The Navy made a multiyear financial commitment in 1982 when I convinced Secretary of the Navy John Lehman that our proposed technology system would provide the United States Navy with the opportunity to find and recover objects of interest from under the sea. Such an advantage held great appeal at the height of the Cold War. The Navy provided the patronage to develop the *Argo-Jason* system and gave it a shakedown cruise during the expeditions to *Thresher* and *Scorpion*.

Our patrons agreed to stay the course, even when many observers called our ideas farfetched, even when there were a few glitches along the way. Nobody mistook a setback for a fatal error. We always pushed ahead.

By 1989 we had a new pair of ROVs ready for a shakedown cruise in the Mediterranean. The small, mobile, tethered robot, *Jason,* was ready to claim its rightful place in ocean exploration history. Its partner was a towed platform that we christened *Hugo,* short for "Huge Argo." Four times the size of *Argo* and weighing 10,000 pounds in air, *Hugo* dwarfed all other underwater vehicles. Its huge box, constructed of aluminum I-beams, made it durable but heavy in water, about 7,000 pounds. It put quite a load on the cable that lowered and raised it.

For *Hugo* and *Jason's* visit to an amphorae-strewn site on the bed of the Mediterranean Sea that April, we added one more element to the vision. Why not share our discoveries in real time with children and teenagers, too? They could go to museums and other sites receiving the satellite downlink and watch the exploration of the seafloor.

I have long been a fan of mythologist Joseph Campbell, who traced the myth of the hero who travels beyond the commonplace and into a world of wonders, encounters fabulous forces, then

sites piped the images to giant television screens so viewers could experience them just as we did. Live audio allowed students to pose questions to us during the 84 real-time broadcasts in the spring of 1989. In all, a quarter-million youth shared our thrills and frustrations.

Only a handful of people saw our biggest setback. During a rehearsal, I had barely said "Good morning from the Mediterranean" when disaster

"HOW I LONGED FOR A SINGLE NEAR VIEW, OR TELESCOPIC EYES WHICH COULD PIERCE THE MURK. I FELT AS IF SOME ASTONISHING DISCOVERY LAY JUST BEYOND THE POWER OF MY EYES."
—UNDERSEA EXPLORER WILLIAM BEEBE, 1931

returns to share his newfound knowledge with his people. Surely our trips to the ocean floor, overcoming enormous obstacles along the way, needed that final element of sharing what we found with those who stayed behind. We must be dreamers, and we must inspire the dreams of others.

And so we began the JASON Project, a series of live broadcasts to North American museums and research centers, 12 at first. Managers at the

struck. *Hugo* was being launched with *Jason* inside. A big wave pushed up our ship's stern just as the massive towed sled began its descent. The cable, which had been slack for a moment, instantly snapped tight and broke, sending *Hugo* to the bottom. I yelped, threw down my headset, and ran from the control van onto the deck.

We recovered *Hugo* but never used it again. It was just too big and heavy, too likely to repeat the

Argus: Towed video/illumination sled with strong lights, top left, tethers to *Hercules* or *Little Hercules*. Hangs from the surface vessel by a fiber-optic cable. Responds to surface motions, but does not transmit them to ROVs. Steered by moving the ship or the cable. Rotated or stabilized by thrusters.

Argo: Advance-scouting eyeball, left, to pair with *Jason*. Unmanned vehicle with video equipment; towed above the ocean floor by a long, fiber-optic cable. Had two sonar systems, forward- and side-looking, and five video cameras. Operated from a van on the surface ship. Found *Titanic*.

Hugo: Second, larger version of *Argo* intended to house *Jason* but quickly abandoned because of handling difficulties. Stands for "huge *Argo*."

EXPLORATION EQUIPMENT

Alvin: Submersible, left, developed by the Office of Naval Research in 1964, takes its name from advocate Al Vine. First dove to 6,000 feet but later to 16,000 feet with a titanium alloy hull introduced in 1974.

ANGUS: Acoustically Navigated Geological Underwater Survey vehicle, also known as "dope on a rope." Had to be retrieved in order for its still-frame photographs to be developed and printed.

Jason Junior: Known as a "swimming eyeball" for its freedom of movement and array of video and still cameras and lights. Small prototype of *Jason* and all ROVs that followed, it was tethered to *Alvin* during close inspection of *Titanic* in 1986. Later lost in a Galapagos expedition.

Jason: Workhorse of undersea exploration, possessing sensitive navigation equipment, thrusters, sonar, cameras, lights, and mechanical arm. Designed for close inspection of sea floor and retrieval of artifacts.

Little Hercules: Shoots high-definition video of shipwrecks and artifacts. Operated from a control van on a surface ship, where pilot can use four thrusters to maneuver it at the end of a 100-foot tether connected to *Argus.* Unlike *Hercules,* can fit inside small openings in shipwrecks. Moves effortlessly in three dimensions.

Hercules: Designed for deep-sea archaeological excavation, left, but suits primarily photographic missions. Has controls, lights, and cameras similar to *Little Herc's*, plus two powerful yet sensitive manipulator arms. Initial deployment at sea during 2003 expeditions to the Black Sea and Mediterranean.

Orpheus: Permanently installed vehicle travels along a wire between fixed points in response to distant commands. Provides live video feeds via Internet2 from the National Marine Sanctuary in Monterey Bay. Similar vehicles planned for other sanctuaries. Demonstrates dream of ROV near *Titanic* to create an underwater museum accessed through telepresence.

Knorr: Research ship operated by the Woods Hole Oceanographic Institution (WHOI). Video from *Argo* deployed from *Knorr* during joint French-American *Titanic* expedition in 1985 gave the world the first view of the ocean liner since 1912.

Atlantis II: WHOI research vessel, retired in 1996 after 34 years of ocean exploration. Surface ship during *Alvin* and *Jason Junior* exploration of *Titanic* in 1986.

Ronald H. Brown: Flagship of the NOAA fleet, commissioned in 1997. State-of-the-art oceanographic and atmospheric research vessel that served as surface platform for 2004 expedition to *Titanic.*

snap-load disaster. We substituted another, lighter relay vehicle, *Medea,* named for the wife of the mythological Jason. And we decided we would launch towed sleds and ROVs separately.

The following year, 1990, found us in Lake Ontario for the second JASON Project, mapping the remains of *Hamilton* and *Scourge,* two American warships from the War of 1812. Telepresence again placed the underwater world before thousands of students. We used a digital still camera on *Jason* to snap a series of pictures during several runs over the two shipwrecks. Our imaging technician stitched the pictures together to create a seamless mosaic while still above the site—a plan we hoped to duplicate above *Titanic.*

As each broadcast from Lake Ontario ended, our *Jason* let a student at a remote site use a joystick and computer display to pilot *Jason,* a compelling demonstration of the practicality of our system. If a youth could interact with ROVs, so could a scientist. And in fact, scientists got their chance in 1993, when we explored hydrothermal vents in the Guaymas Basin in the Gulf of California. They shared in the data we collected, then directed our crew to collect certain biological samples and make specific water temperature measurements.

Since then, there have been many annual JASON Project voyages, funded by a variety of organizations and government agencies, and long-distance scientific investigations along the coast of Belize, and in the Galapagos Islands, Iceland, Yellowstone National Park, Hawaii, and the Florida Keys. During the 2004 *Titanic* voyage, a JASON Math Adventure instructed sixth- through eighth-graders in the geometry basic to the exploration.

IT'S ONE THING to voyage to a shipwreck and set up a temporary broadcast. It's another to make the broadcast live and continuous. That's the ultimate vision, and challenge, that I see for *Titanic.* Imagine the ship turned into a museum, right on the ocean floor. Not a museum with walls and glass and little white cards that describe curios and antiques, but a museum that is a real site, accessed through telepresence nonetheless. It would be a museum where anyone with access to a computer and a browser could log on, click a few keys, and tour the ship in real time. It would be the ultimate application of technology to make the distant seem close.

Here are the steps to get there:

First, scientists would have to thoroughly survey and evaluate the shipwreck. That was the first phase of our 2004 expedition. The next step requires important decisions that are by and large out of our hands. The governments of Britain, America, France, and Canada could choose to preserve *Titanic* in situ, using a combination of international accords to regulate visitation and scientific preservation methods to retard, stop, or even reverse the decay. Already the oil and gas industry possesses the automated machinery to scrape and paint ships below the waterline, something routinely done for the hulls of supertankers. It could be done to *Titanic,* too.

If all four governments of these North Atlantic nations agree to a protocol of preservation—the U.S. and Britain already have—the final step would be for some kind of ROVs to be installed around and possibly inside *Titanic.* Each would have the necessary cameras, lights, and operating systems. Where would you like to go? Care to see the Turkish bath? Click-click, and you send a robot down a control wire into the steamroom. Want to tour the captain's quarters or the Grand Staircase? Click-click, and there you are. Or how about Molly Brown's suite? You're there before you can say "mousepad." Better still, imagine having multiple cameras and multiple robotic systems to maneuver them. You then would have a wealth of choices.

The virtual museum's electronic components

JACQUES PICCARD *and Don Walsh wave from* Trieste *after conquering Challenger Deep in 1960.*

could be connected to a surface buoy or ship by cable, their signal then relayed to a satellite. The cable need only be a little over 12,000 feet long, the distance from the White House to the Pentagon. Or the signal could be patched into one of the transatlantic cables that snake along the bottom nearby. I'm not exactly sure of all the details of a *Titanic* museum. I only know that it will be grand.

The technology is already in use. The Immersion Institute, created by Mystic Aquarium and the Institute for Exploration with NOAA's help, is wiring our 13 National Marine Sanctuaries. These underwater parks lie along continental America's coastline and in the waters of Hawaii, American Samoa, and Lake Huron. The Immersion Project plans to bring one on line each year.

First was the Monterey Bay sanctuary, at more than 5,300 square miles the largest in the continental U.S. For three years, live feeds from two underwater and two surface cameras at the bay have been streaming video. Some might scoff and say the California coast isn't the bottom of the Atlantic—and they would be right. It's worse. *Titanic's* environment is a quiet moonscape comparatively. In Monterey Bay, huge storms churn up the water, strong currents push against the ROV we call *Orpheus,* and barnacles seem determined to

LITTLE HERCULES, *tethered to the* Northern Horizon, *begins a dive during the Black Sea Project, exploring sites near the Turkish port of Sinop.*

attach themselves to the cameras. Still, for many months I have watched live video of Monterey Bay from my office in Connecticut via Internet2.

One of the cameras on the edge of the bay looks out over the water, its back to Cannery Row. I've daydreamed of sending a command across the continent to turn the camera around and watch the human parade on shore. Imagine: You see a mugging. You call 911 in California. You say, "I want to report a crime." The voice on the line asks, "Where are you?" and you reply, "I'm in Mystic, Connecticut."

The next logical step will be to bring a cultural site online in a marine sanctuary. That's the plan for Thunder Bay in Lake Huron, where about 160 shipwrecks litter the bottom. It's a little trickier there because of the relative difficulty in hooking up the Internet2 feed, but it can be done. Just wait.

The unresolved questions about *Titanic*'s future center on our will and our finances. We have to want to preserve the grand old ship. We have to agree on a way to do it. And we have to pay for it.

How long will it be before this dream is realized? I don't know. I only know that we must take the first step.

It's time to return to *Titanic*. ■

AS I ENDED *my 2003 search for ancient shipwrecks in the Black Sea, I planned to revisit the modern* Titanic. *The oceans hold a wealth of history to explore and share.*

THE PROMENADE

When Olympic put to sea, first-class passengers complained that its open promenade deck exposed them to sea spray during rough weather. As a result, just before Titanic's launch, Harland & Wolff installed windows to shelter the forward two-fifths of its promenade deck from the elements. The altered promenade and open boat deck above it became favorite places for a stroll. As Titanic sank, these decks became crowded with panicking passengers. In contrast, Isidor and Ida Straus, above, calmly settled into deck chairs to await their deaths together. The portside lower and upper promenade decks, left, now lie in silent darkness.

RUSTICLE-ENCRUSTED, *the davit for Lifeboat No. 8, above, which Ida Straus refused to enter after her husband was turned away, remains in the cranked-out position on the port boat deck. The lifeboat, which had a capacity of 65, went into the water with 28 aboard, including Ida Straus's maid, Ellen Bird.*

PASSENGERS WALK *Titanic's deck, right. Although a Harland & Wolff executive urged twice the number of lifeboats, White Star decision makers believed* Titanic *would be its own lifeboat.*

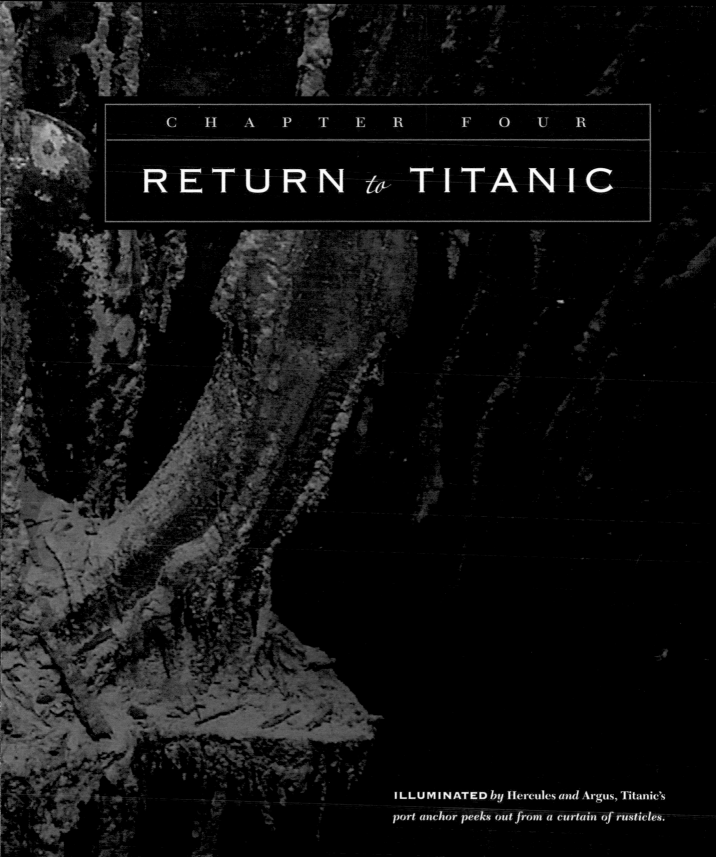

CHAPTER FOUR
RETURN *to* TITANIC

ILLUMINATED *by* Hercules *and* Argus, Titanic's
port anchor peeks out from a curtain of rusticles.

TIED UP AT THE PIER, directly beyond a security gate, the NOAA state-of-the-art flagship *Ronald H. Brown* stood ready for our voyage, ready to stretch the frontiers of science and show the world the possibilities of telepresence.

Over the next 17 days, our expedition would bring together the best in the deep-submergence community, including experts in navigation, communications, and video technology. That combination, we hoped, would resonate emotionally with those on board and with viewers worldwide. In addition to live JASON and Immersion Project webcasts, 11 days into the expedition the National Geographic Channel was scheduled to broadcast an hour-long program, *Return to Titanic*. It would include a live video feed from the shipwreck. The Channel promoted the show in advance, to build an audience. All of our new technology would have

to deliver on time, as advertised, regardless of mechanical glitches, bad weather, or whatever else an unpredictable cruise in the North Atlantic could throw at us. Talk about pressure.

The *Ron Brown* carried a crew of 26 and 32 passengers including scientists, engineers, technicians, a video production team, and others who would document the voyage and create portions of the broadcast. Many were old hands on my expeditions and familiar with the Institute for Exploration: Jim Newman, a University of Rhode Island consultant who designed *Hercules* and *Little Hercules*, and Dave Lovalvo, the founder and

---

JUNE 3, 2004, *was one of those rare days in the North Atlantic, brilliant with sunshine, blue skies, and calm seas. Here, aboard the* Ronald H. Brown, *we hover above the site of the shipwreck* Titanic.

owner of Eastern Oceanics, who has been piloting submersibles and ROVs for three decades. Dave wears coveralls even when he's not tinkering. *Hercules's* pilots included two employees from the university: the curly-haired engineer Todd Gregory, who oversaw the ROV's mechanics and hydraulics, and the goateed and pony-tailed technician Tom Orvosh. At the controls of the towed sled *Argus* would be the Institute for Exploration's chief boatswain, Mark DeRoche, consultant and skilled technician from the University of Rhode Island; his fellow technician Dave Wright, a self-described "shade tree mechanic"; and computer engineering student Webb Pinner, whose first name is really John but who seems to think Webb works better for an Internet wizard.

My right hand, assistant chief scientist and URI researcher Dwight Coleman, brought expertise in oceanography and marine geology and would take care of the expedition's day-to-day logistics. Also with us was a friend, Capt. Craig McLean, who directs NOAA's Office of Ocean Exploration. Craig combines a fanatic's knowledge of the *Titanic* with an advocate's passion for preserving it. Working with lawyers, scientists, diplomats, and bureaucrats for a decade, Craig helped get the U.S. and other nations to agree on a protocol to preserve *Titanic*, regulate visits to the shipwreck, and punish those who mistreat the great gray lady under the Atlantic.

The morning of Thursday, May 27, 2004, dawned cool, overcast, and gray. A low-pressure system squatted off the coast of Newfoundland, several hundred miles to the northeast, and refused to move. It spun off unusually wintry weather toward New England and pitched storms out into the Atlantic. The forecast for the site of the *Titanic* shipwreck, one thousand miles east of Boston, called for 10- to 12-foot seas by May 30, our scheduled arrival date. One of my biggest fears for this trip looked as if it might come true.

It would take us a little more than three days to get to *Titanic's* grave, and about the same time to get back. With government sponsors, we had to follow a government timetable. Six travel days left only eleven days on site. If the low-pressure system didn't move, it might kick up gale-force winds and build up the seas. Stormy weather could prevent us from launching or recovering *Argus* and *Hercules*, since they might bang catastrophically against the side of the ship, get sucked into the stern propellers, or rise and fall so suddenly it could damage their tethers. I had allowed for two days of bad weather in our itinerary—but what if the North Atlantic refused to cooperate? Our plans for a return to *Titanic* could turn into nothing more than a topside sightseeing tour of foam-crested waves and storm clouds.

I could only hope for the best. There's no use getting anxious about things you cannot control. On land, I am driven to complete task after task in pursuit of a goal. But at sea, the winds and waves set the pace. The sea has a way of building patience—

DWIGHT COLEMAN, *left, and I examine* Hercules *on the deck of the* Ron Brown *before leaving Boston Harbor.*

after all, can you imagine anywhere on land where you would be happy traveling day after day at 12 to 15 miles per hour, the *Ron Brown's* cruising speed?

I walked around and inspected the ship. It reminded me a lot of the *Knorr*, right down to the arrangement of the chief scientist's cabin. It was clean, powerful, and comfortable, although not particularly flashy. It was, after all, a science ship run by the Department of Commerce.

Down three decks from my cabin were the many laboratories set up to record and analyze data collected during dives. An electronics lab

contained computer consoles that registered the ship's movements, recorded the depth of the ocean beneath the ship, and mapped the bottom. A five-foot model of *Titanic*, set up in the lab, would help orient us as we explored the shipwreck.

To one side of the electronics lab was a hydro lab with more computer equipment, to the other side a jury-rigged TV production studio. Across the passageway was the main lab, where we would have meetings, shoot segments for the JASON webcasts, and watch ongoing dives on a 52-inch monitor, wired to the control van on the stern deck.

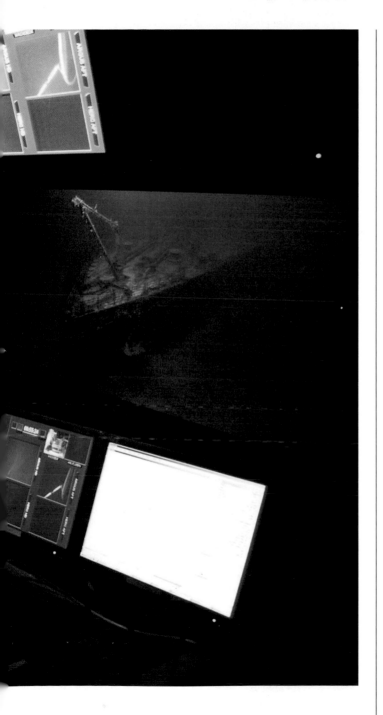

The control van was nothing more than two shipping containers, connected lengthwise, with an opening cut in the center wall. Electronics filled nearly every square inch of the port side of the van, a series of workstations connected to a communications network by headset microphones. First came the navigator, who would monitor the location of *Argus* and *Hercules* relative to *Titanic* and ask the ship's bridge to reposition the *Ron Brown* to shift the vehicles below. To the navigator's left sat the *Hercules* pilot, and to his left, the *Argus* pilot. The *Herc* pilot's joysticks controlled thrusters that moved the ROV in three-dimensional space. *Herc*'s clever Doppler navigational system continually sent pings from the four corners of its undercarriage down to the underlying terrain, then plotted the vehicle's position according to the echoes.

Argus's pilot had less control. The towed sled moved when its cable was raised or lowered or when the mother ship repositioned. About all the *Argus* pilot could do, besides calling for surface adjustments, was to spin the sled to reposition its cameras and lights, which served as *Hercules*'s lighting platform. Both pilots had to keep an eye on the distance between their vehicles so the tether between them stayed slack and untangled.

VIDEO IMAGES *from* Argus, *shaded blue, and from* Hercules, *clearer, at right,* allow NOAA scientist Catalina Martinez and me to study Titanic *from the control van.*

In front of the navigator and the two pilots were three plasma screens. Usually one screen showed *Hercules*'s high-definition video, another a similar video from *Argus*, and the third miniatures of all available video views. These included live images from the winch deck on the *Ron Brown*'s stern, the aft cameras for both *Argus* and *Herc*, images from bubble cameras inside and on top of *Herc*, and utility cameras to help navigate. A video operator selected and recorded images, zoomed and focused the various cameras, and changed tapes.

On the starboard side of the van, the leaders of the three watches could take turns directing the entire operation. We designated a seat in the back for a data logger, who would record information from the dives and capture still-frame images from the high-definition video. And there was a third seat for me. Once we reached *Titanic*, I expected to be in the van nearly every waking moment.

The control van had no windows, but the plasma screens displaying images from the ocean floor would be our looking glass on the underwater world. The self-contained universe of the

LIFTED *by a crane off the deck of the* Ron Brown, Hercules *is positioned for immersion and its first descent to* Titanic. *At left, wearing a yellow jacket, I lend a hand.*

command and control van stayed dark, quiet, and surprisingly cold, due to some glitch in the air-conditioning system. It provided a touch of verisimilitude: The water around *Titanic* is about 2°C, and the ship sank on a sub-freezing night. Visitors ought to shiver a little.

The van's interior could pass for something out of a rocket-to-Mars movie. The port shipping container, which held the vehicle control equipment, cost about $1 million. The back half, where images were displayed on plasma screens, cost $25,000—cheap enough to put copies in science centers around the world. An observer thousands of miles away in a duplicate command center could see the same image and take control of the exploration. An audio component allowed for two-way conversation.

I wandered outside the van and onto the fantail. There sat the workhorses of the expedition. *Hercules* perched atop a platform bolted to the deck. In the three weeks before our sailing date, the seven-foot-tall, boxy ROV had completed a test run aboard the *Ron Brown*. Jim Newman thought the initial voyage would offer us a good chance to get the bugs out of *Hercules* and *Argus* before the more pressure-filled trip to *Titanic*. *Hercules* had never been tested at *Titanic*'s depth. In fact, during its trial expedition to the coral-covered Mountains in the Sea southeast of Massachusetts, *Hercules* suffered a minor hydraulic breakdown. The engineers had trouble fixing it until the *Ron Brown*'s chief boatswain, Bruce Cowden, who proved to be a jovial yet thoughtful man, carved them a good-luck charm.

Also on the stern were a crane for lowering *Hercules* into the water, an A-frame to do the same for *Argus*, and a Dynacon winch wound with 2.5 miles of cable with a fiber-optic core—enough, I was assured, to drop *Herc* and *Argus* down to *Titanic* and still have a layer of cable on its spool. But what if the cable was bowed too much by the current as the vehicles descended, or if the vehicles strayed from the surface ship? It was too late now for second thoughts. The cable would reach *Titanic* or it would not.

Argus sat lashed to the fantail, inches from the edge. The size and shape of a small, low-slung car, it would be lowered directly into the water and sink like a cinder block. We hoped we had built it tough

TUGBOATS, *including one named* Hercules, *guide* Titanic *down the Belfast Lough for sea trials.*

enough to withstand the up-and-down jerking of its cable as the *Ron Brown* responded to swells and waves. *Argus* hadn't experienced anything like the nasty weather the North Atlantic can dish out, and we had our fingers crossed that it would not have to.

Next to *Argus*, on the starboard side of the stern, rested another shipping container, our main toolshed—virtually a small hardware store. We knew that something would go wrong mechanically on this voyage. Something always does.

A 98-foot umbilical cord connected *Hercules* with *Argus*. It relayed electrical power down and received video images back. The key was to keep that tether slack. If the tether were to be pulled tight, the effect would be like cracking a bullwhip. Too much whipsawing might kink or snap the tether, breaking its internal optical filaments and rendering *Herc* deaf, blind, and mute. We attached a "football" of syntactic foam on the cable between *Herc* to *Argus*, hoping it would maintain enough slack to absorb surface motions.

Another shipping container, jarringly aquagreen against the ship's white paint, rested below

PORING OVER *debris-field sketches, the science crew plots our exploration strategy. At right are archaeology graduate student Katy Croff and NOAA Capt. Craig McLean.*

and in front of the bridge. Inside, communications engineer Scott Stamps of EDS Corp. would be the crucial link in the plan to share our voyage in real time with the world. His computer equipment would take the electronic images from *Titanic* and relay their signals to EDS's headquarters in Plano, Texas, which then would convert them to Internet protocol and distribute them. Viewers watching at Internet2 sites could respond in real time, asking questions of the science team, thanks to one satellite in geostationary orbit and an antenna atop the control van programmed to point at it no matter how crazily the ship twisted and dipped with the waves, and to a second satellite that received the signals converted at EDS headquarters in Plano.

Slowly, groups began to gather in the main lab and the electronics lab. I studied a sketch of the *Titanic* site and debris field created from the notes of marine scientist Al Uchupi, a geomorphologist, in 1986. The sketch gave us a starting point. It indicated positions of *Titanic*'s bow and stern and items in the debris field. But it was based on 20-year-old technology, from the time when global positioning technology was only good to within ten meters. I also had a blown-up, monochromatic photomosaic of *Titanic's* bow section, from the October 1987 issue of NATIONAL GEOGRAPHIC. The mosaic had been assembled from 108 black-and-white photographs and tinted ocean-blue. One of our missions was for *Hercules* to remap *Titanic* using downward-looking, digital-imaging system

we would not be able to explore the interior of *Titanic*. He did have some upbeat news, though: The State Department was close to approving the international treaty to protect *Titanic*—the same treaty that Britain had signed months earlier. "It is possible for the treaty to be signed while we're out here," he said. It would be dramatic news indeed, if we could not only show the world how

"THERE'S NOT A LOT OF HISTORICAL OR ARCHAEOLOGICAL KNOWLEDGE WE COULD GET [FROM *TITANIC*], BUT THERE'S A HECK OF A LOT TO LEARN ABOUT SCIENCE .... *TITANIC* IS A GREAT TESTBED FOR ANALYZING SHIPWRECKS."

—NOAA Lt. JEREMY WEIRICH,
ON THE 2004 EXPEDITION

software to generate a high-tech mosaic. Scientists could compare new and old to see two decades of change in *Titanic*.

Once everyone was on board, the *Ron Brown* pulled away from the pier. It was 10:35 a.m. Our next stop: one thousand miles nearly due east. Our speed: 12 knots. Patience, indeed. The first two days passed slowly. We called a general meeting in the main lab to learn ship's routines and each other's names. That's when Craig told the science crew that

Titanic has suffered but also announce our government's commitment to saving it.

THICK FOG SURROUNDED US that first night at sea. The horn bellowed to alert nearby fishing vessels of our presence. The ship found a current in the Gulf Stream and picked up speed to 13 knots. The weather stayed gray, with a gentle rain that began on Friday and

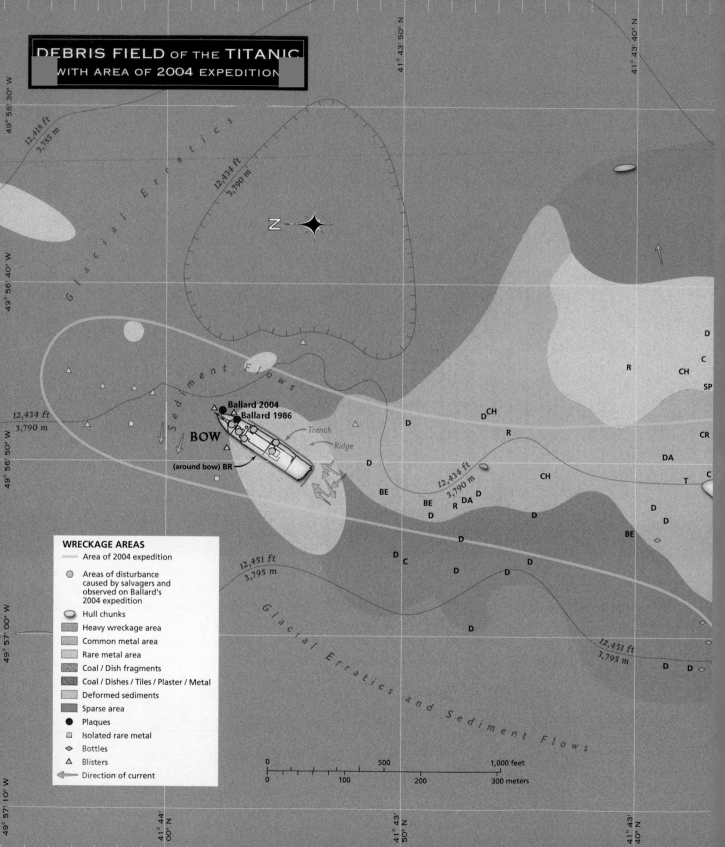

DEBRIS FIELD OF THE TITANIC
WITH AREA OF 2004 EXPEDITION

49° 55' 30" W
49° 56' 40" W
49° 56' 50" W
49° 57' 00" W
49° 57' 10" W

41° 43' 50" N
41° 43' 40" N
41° 44' 00" N
41° 43' 50" N
41° 43' 40" N

12,418 ft
3,785 m

12,434 ft
3,790 m

12,434 ft
3,790 m

12,434 ft
3,790 m

12,451 ft
3,795 m

12,451 ft
3,795 m

Glacial Erratics

Sediment Flows

Glacial Erratics and Sediment Flows

N

Ballard 2004
Ballard 1986

BOW

(around bow) BR

Trench

Ridge

D
R
C
CH
SP
CR
DA
T
C
BE
BE
D
R
DA
D
D
D
CH
CH
D
D
D
C
D
D
D
D
D
BE
D
D
D
R
D CH
D

WRECKAGE AREAS

— Area of 2004 expedition

○ Areas of disturbance caused by salvagers and observed on Ballard's 2004 expedition

⬭ Hull chunks

▦ Heavy wreckage area

▦ Common metal area

▦ Rare metal area

▦ Coal / Dish fragments

▦ Coal / Dishes / Tiles / Plaster / Metal

▦ Deformed sediments

▦ Sparse area

● Plaques

□ Isolated rare metal

◇ Bottles

△ Blisters

← Direction of current

0   500   1,000 feet

0   100   200   300 meters

WRECKAGE ARTIFACTS

AR	Air scoop	CH	Chamber pot	FB	Funnel base No. 4	R	Railing	TE	Telephone
B	Boiler	CN	Condenser	FD	Feed filter	RE	Refrigerator engine	TI	Tile
BE	Bed springs and posts	CO	Coils	G	Galley section	S	Safe	TO	Toilet
BL	Balustrade	CR	Crane	LP	Low pressure cylinder	SH	Shoe	W	Window frame
BR	Rusticle fragments	D	Dishes / Dish fragments		(Reciprocating Engine)	SMC	Smoking room ceiling	WA	Wash basin
BT	Bathtub	DA	Davit	M	Milk jugs	SP	Stack pipes	WFP	Whistle, Funnel pieces
C	Compass	EV	Evaporator	PD	Port deck section	SW	Ship's wheel		
CA	Catwalk	F	Possible funnel section	PW	Poop wheel	T	Telegraph		

49° 56' 30" W
49° 56' 40" W

12,418 ft
3,785 m

12,418 ft
3,785 m

12,434 ft
3,790 m

3,790 m

12,434 ft

WFP
CH
C
CH
CA
C
RE
CA
CA
CA
CO
TO
SP
EV
C
T
BL SP
SP
TO
AR
SW
PW
LP SH
B
RE
R
BE CH
AR
PW
AR
S
G SMC
SMC
TE
B
TO
FD
BT
PD
C
AR
D WA
BL
BT
BE
CA
B
FD
BL
CR
FB
CH
M S
12,451 ft
3,795 m
BE
R
LP
WO
CR
BE
CR
Cameron
2001
CR
S
CR
TO
CA
BE

STERN

Ballard
1986
(removed)
BR (around stern)
W
CN
CH
F
BE
S
CO
CH
BE
CO
D
BE
S
CH
BL
CH
D

D

BE
BE
D
BE
BE
D R
TI
BE

D

R

CH

CH

D

CH

DEBRIS *from the broken sections of* Titanic *scattered across the ocean floor, providing information about the ship's interior without the need for opening the hull. The current–aided distribution pattern helped us pinpoint the bow in 1985.*

41° 43' 30" N
41° 43' 20" N
41° 43' 10" N

49° 57' 00" W
49° 57' 10" W

came and went for 48 hours. Weather is unpredictable in the North Atlantic, and we began receiving conflicting reports about what lay ahead. One said seas were running high at the *Titanic* site but were expected to calm by the time we were to arrive, around noon on Sunday. A few hours later, ship's Capt. Tim Wright gave us a new forecast: eight-foot seas and 30-knot winds on the ocean surface Sunday above the shipwreck. The captain said he had put equipment over the side in worse weather, but none so expensive as *Argus* and *Hercules*. That night, dolphins played in the ship's bow wake—a good sign.

I spent much of Saturday afternoon in my cabin, listening to a CD of Vladimir Horowitz on the piano and putting together a custom-made jigsaw puzzle of *Titanic*. The puzzle box rested on a stand in my cabin, next to a bronze plaque, an exact copy of the tribute that is now gone—perhaps removed— from *Titanic*'s stern. As the "no-touch" rules prevented us from leaving it on the ship itself, my plan was to place it near the bow. I felt confident that all the work that could be done had been done. I was relaxing for what I knew would be the last chance for a long time.

Miraculously, the sun came out Sunday morning, but the rough seas concerned me. As we approached Titanic Canyon, the small valley off the

PIECING TOGETHER *a custom-made jigsaw puzzle of the R.M.S.* Titanic *was one way to relax and yet still ponder the grandeur of the sunken ocean liner.*

Grand Banks where the ship came to rest, Dwight Coleman began mapping the ocean floor. The *Ron Brown's* SeaBeam bathymetric scanner sent out a ping every few seconds in a six- to seven-mile-wide arc beneath the ship. Unlike the single-beam system I had used in the 1980s, this new "multibeam" program took several measurements at once, under the ship, to port, and to starboard. A computer analyzed the echo and produced a color-coded map of the landscape surrounding *Titanic*.

The hundreds of square miles we hoped to map would take days. In fact, mapping occupied our time whenever *Hercules* and *Argus* were out of water. The ship would "mow the lawn," tracking east-west grid lines at about 8 to 10 knots, and gradually fill in the map's blank spaces with reds, yellows, and greens coded to indicate depth. The finished product conceivably could help future marine archaeologists in two ways. First, greater knowledge about currents and geology at the

SILHOUETTED *by sunset, Scott Stamps of EDS Corp. adjusts the satellite antenna.*

Titanic site could improve predictions about the ship's future. *Titanic* sits at the edge of what essentially is an underwater river valley churning with fast, abrasive flows coming off the eastern shore of Canada. Landslides pose a risk, and in fact a massive undersea slide did occur nearby in 1929. It was not until our French-American team found *Titanic* in 1985 that we were sure it had not been buried.

The second potential advantage of the map lay in applying *Titanic*'s lessons to other shipwrecks. Despite the practical knowledge we have gained one expedition at a time, there is no theory to explain why some shipwrecks survive nearly untouched and others vanish. *Titanic* is a terrific "test bed," given its dramatically different bow, stern, and debris areas, subjected to similar oceanic conditions.

"We are now one mile from the wreck site," the ship's address system boomed at 12:34 p.m. ET May 30. "Nothing goes over the side from this point on." We didn't want any garbage landing on *Titanic* or its debris field.

A small crowd gathered in the electronics lab to watch the sub bottom-profiler, a sophisticated echo sounder, as it delineated the sea floor beneath us. At 12:43, the ship passed over *Titanic*'s bow. The profiler's monitor drew a peanut-shaped bump above the gentle curve of the ocean floor. In the computer's color coding system, the floor appeared as a matrix of yellow and green dots, while the ship showed purple. Everyone marveled at that violet spot and what it represented.

I checked the weather. Still sunny, and calmer than had been predicted. "All right, everybody, let's go to launch position," I called out. The science crew members scrambled to their stations in the control van and on the stern. Officers on the bridge swung the ship's bow 180 degrees so it faced west and engaged the dynamic position system's one bow and two stern propellers to lock us in place. In that orientation, the ocean's five- to seven-foot waves lapped against the bow at a 45-degree angle, creating what sailors call a "quartering sea." The ship rested easy, neither rising up and down on the waves, nor wallowing in their troughs.

Bruce Cowden pulled the levers to lift *Hercules* off its pad, swing it over the port rail, and gently drop it into the water. Blue water and white bubbles danced across our control van's video monitors as the ROV's pilot drove it inches below the surface in a semicircular path toward the stern. The A-frame, leaning out over the ocean, picked up the 4,000-pound *Argus* like a toy and dropped it unceremoniously into the water beside *Hercules*. The control van gave a thumbs-up, and as the winch operator began paying out *Argus*'s 2.5-mile cable, *Hercules*'s pilot began sending it down, using its top-mounted thrusters. Both vehicles began a four-hour descent to the bow section. It was 1:40 p.m.

The descent tends to be rather monotonous. The lights of the ROV and towed sled illuminate the pitch-black waters, turning them shades from cerulean to royal blue. The occasional shrimp or fish

The *M* stood for mail. R.M.S.—Royal Mail Steamer—*Titanic* had a post office with a sorting room on the starboard G deck and a storage room just below on the orlop deck. During the maiden voyage, three American clerks and two British clerks processed mail bound from Europe to the United States. The ship took on 3,364 bags of mail, or approximately 400,000 letters, from Southampton, Cherbourg, and Queenstown. As they sailed west, passengers and crew posted their own cards and letters, adding to the total. A few, like the postcard shown here, were delivered to European ports of call before *Titanic* set off across the Atlantic. They reached their destinations. Many who wrote them never did.

The clerks had intended to have it all sorted before *Titanic* arrived in New York. They took a break on the evening of April 14 to celebrate with American clerk Oscar S. Woody, whose 44th birthday fell the next day. A short time later, the iceberg smashed into the hull not far away. The five postal workers were among the first to understand the magnitude of the damage. Seawater poured into the orlop deck,

THE MAIL CLERKS

soaking more than 200 bags of registered mail in the storage room and forcing two clerks to ascend to the sorting room. The water rose, sloshed onto G deck, and kept going from front to back.

A few minutes after the collision, Fourth Officer Joseph Boxhall, Assistant Second Class Steward Joseph Wheat, whose room was nearby, and Capt. Edward J. Smith examined the sorting room from the vantage of F deck, one flight up. "I looked through an open door and saw these men working at the [mail] racks, and directly beneath me was the mail hold, and the water seemed to be then within 2 feet of the deck we were standing on," Boxhall told an American board of inquiry. The clerks returned to their posts to try to save the mail, but their efforts proved futile. Like the musicians in the ship's orchestra, who did their duty as long as they could and died to the last man, the mail clerks all perished.

During the 2004 expedition, *Hercules* found a "LETTERS" sign faceup in the sediment near the broken bow. Fittingly, the bottom of the Atlantic was the final destination for nearly all mail on the ship. It is also the final resting place of Oscar Woody, one of the American clerks, found a week after the disaster, mail routing slips still in his pocket. The slips were removed and the body buried at sea.

glides past the cameras. Bubbles and organic particles of "sea snow" flit across the screen. A succession of eight-inch squid, whitish and ghostly, squirt their ink and get out of the way as the vehicles approach. Other than that, standing at the video monitor was like watching the sun pass across a cloudless sky. Some crew members used the time to do their laundry or exercises. Not me. I had waited 18 years to return to *Titanic*. I was not about to miss a minute of it.

At 5:42, a lumpy, tan, seemingly endless plain loomed in *Hercules's* cameras. It was the bottom of the North Atlantic, sculpted by currents, *Titanic's* thunderous impact, sea snow, and glacial erratics, rocks left by melting icebergs. The countless bumps resembled miniature sand dunes. Lighter shades of mud eerily resembled human footprints—a phenomenon of sediment accumulation playing a trick on our minds, for nobody could walk here. Submersible tracks, possibly from the Russians' *Mir* I and *Mir* II or the French *Nautile*, crisscrossed the field. The depth indicator registered 12,365 feet. The winch's gauge said it had spooled out 3,801 meters (12,470 feet) of cable. We had made it to the bottom with cable to spare—but not much!

We could see *Hercules's* shadow on the ocean floor under the lights of *Argus*, which hovered about ten meters above the mud. Reckoning by our old maps, we were 2,383 feet from the bow section. Together, all three vehicles—ship, towed sled, and ROV—began moving southwest at two-tenths

of a knot. The sonar indicated hard targets to the east and in other directions, but we could not be sure which was the bow section. The lights of *Hercules* and *Argus* illuminated a circle about the size of a tennis court. Beyond that, everything was murky or invisible.

Hercules crossed over more glacial erratics. Then it encountered a few lumps of coal—the ship's first calling cards. Tons of unburned coal had spilled when *Titanic* split apart. We had charted some of the major deposits in 1986.

A bright orange shrimp skittered across the mud. We saw a teacup resting on the bottom. Whether it was from *Titanic* or not, we could not say. This part of the ocean has been a major highway between Europe and North America for centuries. The hours slowed to a crawl. The *Ron Brown's* movements were taking longer than I had expected to translate down to *Argus*. Even my patience was getting a bit thin. "I'll be glad when we find this guy and can set up camp," I said at 9:30, more than three hours into our transit across the ocean floor.

As it turned out, we did not have to wait much longer. A large, hard target suddenly dominated the sonar monitor, and debris of obviously human origin began to appear on the video screen. The first substantial piece looked like a davit, the small cranes that lowered the lifeboats. Was it part of *Titanic*, or could it have come from a convoy that passed overhead during World War II? We could not tell. "Let's continue west a little more," I said, "and if we have a bias, let's go north."

At 10:22, *Hercules* stumbled upon a large chunk of metal, likely part of an interior bulkhead. We continued onward. Our frustrations began to grow at being so close to *Titanic*, yet so slow to make the final distance. "We're clearly south of the bow," I told the crew in the control van. "We're in the debris field, so we go north, gentlemen."

The debris field is *Titanic*'s poignant signature, a junkyard landscape of personal artifacts that reminds us that it was a ship of human beings. As I pondered these thoughts, a bed rail suddenly appeared in front of *Hercules*. We stared in awe, our imaginations running wild. "Only one person slept in that bed," I whispered. *Titanic* sank on its maiden voyage, after all, so the bed probably had only one occupant for four and a half nights.

A screamer of a target lit up the sonar. It had to be the bow. Nothing else could be so big, so close. The sonar showed that whatever it was, it lay a few dozen meters from *Hercules*. Its shape appeared square and tall. "That's the goodies," I said into the headset. "We want to go there."

Hercules pilot Tom Orvosh broke our collective astonishment to announce that he was having difficulty keeping the ROV at a constant depth. *Herc* seemed heavy, and he had to expend an excessive amount of vertical thrust to keep it off the bottom. A crack in the syntactic foam, sustained during the dive to the Mountains in the Sea, must have

tipped *Hercules*'s buoyancy from slightly positive to slightly negative.

There was nothing we could do other than try to make *Herc* a little lighter and keep the thrusters blasting. We decided that at a convenient time and place, we would empty the bio box, which contained my replacement plaque and a rusticle experiment station that microbiologist Roy Cullimore wanted us to place near the bow. Meanwhile, I told Tom and the rest of the crew that once we got visual confirmation of the bow, we could drop a marker, recover the vehicles, and fix what needed to be fixed before a second dive.

No sooner had I shared those thoughts than the bridge called down to the van with a new weather forecast. In the next six hours, the bridge officer said, we would encounter "a significant sea change." The winds and waves would kick up, forcing us to have *Argus* and *Hercules* safely lashed on deck. *But not before I see what I came for,* I thought.

The sonar target grew larger and cast a shadow behind it. Whatever it was, it was 20 meters away, quite large, and coming into view. Clouds of dust swirled in front of the cameras as the thrusters churned. "Rise up another five meters and see if we can get out of it," I told the pilots. The sediment fell away from *Hercules* like a curtain cut from its rod. "Pivot left, pivot left. Dave, square on it," I told *Argus* pilot Dave Wright. I wanted both *Argus*'s and *Herc*'s lights on the scene before us.

And there, at 11:22, straight in front of *Hercules* and filling the monitor as if right in front of us, not some 13,000 feet below, stood the torn rear section of the bow. "The back end is sandwiched," I said into the headset microphone. Then, excitedly, "That's a boiler!" *Hercules* had come upon the flattened deck plates at the end opposite *Titanic*'s majestic foredeck, the tear itself where the ship ripped in two.

Rectangular doors to the stokehold were plainly visible. The metal had taken on a blue-green patina and a mossy, microbial beard. Above and to the left, brighter, yellow-orange metal, almost glowing like sulfur, topped the boiler like a cocked hat. Freshly exposed metal? We could not be sure. In fact, most of what we saw would take weeks, months, even years to sort out. For now, we just gaped.

We decided to stroll along the port side of the bow section. *Hercules* rose, swung to the left, and floated up to the promenade deck, where many a passenger enjoyed the ocean view. Now that deck looked to be collapsing, from the aft forward. *Herc*'s cameras relayed a yellow mark amid the green, possibly indicating impact damage from a submersible. Its cameras captured porthole after porthole,

A STEAMER TRUNK, *its treated leather unpalatable to microbes, remains remarkably intact.*

Commemorating All Those Lost On
RMS TITANIC

From The People Of
Cobh (Queenstown) And Ireland

Go dTuga Dia Suaimhneas Síoraí
Dá nAnamacha

August 2000

THE BRASS TELEMOTOR, *which once held the ship's wooden wheel, has attracted memorial plaques deposited by visitors.*

window glass still intact, sticking out of a vertical plane of decaying metal, so smeared in greens, oranges, reds, and yellows that it looked like a Jackson Pollock painting. I thought of faces pressed to the glass, looking out as the ship left the ports of Southampton, Cherbourg, and Queenstown.

I felt almost as if I were seeing *Titanic* for the first time. The last time here, I had glimpsed the ship through *Alvin's* softball-sized windows with limited lighting. Now, I saw *Titanic* as if in full sun, through a bay window. There was no comparison. Everything appeared with crystal clarity: hull plates, bow railings, bitts, and those haunting portholes. The view was closer, broader, and more detailed than it had ever been before. If I had had the time, I could have literally seen every inch of *Titanic's* exterior.

Hercules and *Argus* paused at the expansion joint, the gap built into the ship to give its structure flexibility. One foot wide in 1986, the joint now lay open in a deep, V-shaped slash. I could not be sure how far it had grown in 18 years. Rising up and moving forward, we came upon one of the two remaining port lifeboat davits. Bent and encrusted, an almost beautiful gold, it occupied the aft position for the fourth boat from the front, indicating it had been used to lower Lifeboat No. 8.

A chill went through me as I examined the crane up close. I could not look at the davit without thinking of the human dramas played out on this spot. On the port side of the ship as it sank, the rescue operation fell under the orders of Second Officer Charles Lightoller. He had interpreted Capt. E. J. Smith's instructions to "put the women and children in and lower away" to mean that *only* women and children should board the lifeboats. On the starboard side, First Officer William Murdoch came to a different conclusion. He filled the boats with as many women and children as were on hand, then allowed male passengers any remaining seats. As *Titanic* sank, the crew and several male passengers escorted single women and wives into Lifeboat No. 8. A steward, John Hart, deposited a score of women and children into the boat after struggling to bring them from the isolated third-class section of the ship. A young girl, nobody knows who, jumped away and announced, "I've forgotten Jack's picture! I must go back and get it!" She rushed below, risking her life, but returned in time to grab a seat.

As the boat was about to be lowered into the water with 28 on board, Ida and Isidor Straus came upon the scene. Ida began to climb in, then turned and stepped out, declaring that she would not leave her husband. Another passenger encouraged Isidor, the owner of Macy's, saying, "I'm sure no one would object to an old gentleman like yourself getting in." But Isidor refused to be singled out. The couple settled into two deck chairs and awaited their fate. Every time I think about that lifeboat davit, I think of the bravery of Ida Straus, who chose to die with her husband rather than live without him.

We moved on. *Hercules* came to the other remaining port davit, the forward one for Lifeboat

No. 2. Near the chief officer's cabin, it stuck out over the side of the ship as if ready to lower another boat. This was the lifeboat in which Lightoller had discovered a group of men, ready to launch. He threatened them with his revolver, saying, "Get out of here, you damned cowards!" The men fled, not knowing that Lightoller's gun held no bullets. The boat took on 25 women, one man from steerage, three crewmen, and Fourth Officer Joseph Boxhall, whom Captain Smith ordered to take charge. Lifeboat No. 2 became the first to be rescued by *Carpathia*.

As *Hercules* and *Argus* swung around to the bridge, we glimpsed the mast. We were running out of time, given the storm brewing overhead. Still, we had enough for a quick tour of the most romantic part of the great ship. I ordered a new course of "000"—due north—to take us over the bow. Below we could see a cargo opening, gaping black like a giant mouth. Impact marks flashed out as orange

NO. 1 FUNNEL *appears to emit steam, an illusion caused by current rushing through its small opening.*

and yellow ovals where submersibles had bumped or landed on the ship, as distinct as muddy shoe prints on a white carpet.

The waves were building in the coming storm, and the towed sled began to be jerked up by its long cable whenever the ship rose on a big swell. We tried to position *Argus* to take photographs, but it whipsawed up and down. A camera wire and a light came loose. "We're going to recover pretty soon," I told Todd, one of our pilots who doubles as master mechanic. "But I want to get a little time in here, now that we took so long to find this."

Given a little freedom from its relay vehicle, *Hercules* sped around the bow. As if on a sightseeing tour, we watched with awe and chagrin as the brass telemotor on the bridge and two cranes slid all too quickly by the cameras. The anchor windlasses and chains stood out in high relief. The links of the chains looked as if they could still raise a ship's anchor today. More orange and yellow ovals dotted the green. At the edge of the forecastle lay a yellow rod several feet long. It appeared to be made of fiberglass or some other modern material, obviously dropped within the last few years. Then I realized that we had an unobstructed view of portions of the deck. Sections of handrail had fallen away. Either they had lost the fight to degradation,

SADLY SAGGING, Titanic's *once festive promenade deck, with the boat deck above, has noticeably deteriorated since* Alvin's *dives to the shipwreck in 1986.*

or they had been disturbed by human visitors. All I knew for certain was that they had been in place when I saw them last.

The bow itself looked remarkably intact. The hull plates and the prow evoked that majestic sense that *Titanic* might still rise up and limp into New York. Harland & Wolff had built the bow to withstand tremendous pressure as it smashed through waves and swells. It had held together remarkably well. Driven into mud nearly up to its anchors, it had escaped exposure to oxygen. I expect the bow will be one of the last parts of the ship to disappear.

Not so the foremast, which encapsulates the ship's tragic end. This mast from which the lookouts issued warnings has collapsed into the well deck—a fact we already knew. But that did not lessen the tremendous sadness over the loss to the ship, and to history, that we felt when we laid our eyes on it.

I wanted to come back later and explore everything up close. Meanwhile, it was time to get *Hercules* and *Argus* back on deck before the storm hit. We placed the plaque and set the rusticle experiment station on the seafloor, marked the spot for a later return, and headed for the surface. It was 1 a.m.

THREE HOURS LATER, the two vehicles rested safely on the stern. The storm had been a false alarm. The vehicles had spent only two hours on the bottom, but I saw our first dive as a success. We had found and scouted *Titanic*'s bow section. We had locked it into our GPS index. We had learned a few of the fundamentals of operating our exploration vehicles at the end of more than 12,000 feet of cable, including the unexpected degree to which swells on the surface pulled *Argus* up and down, and the half-hour to an hour that it took for the ship's lateral motions to be felt at the ocean floor.

We also had learned something about the North Atlantic's power. Even on a relatively calm day, its surface waves had yanked *Argus* around. Our two vehicles would have to face more vigorous tests than we had thought. I had high expectations for the second dive, though. The previous night's back-and-forth search for *Titanic*'s bow had left a variety of twists in *Argus*'s cable. Now, conceivably, we could drop it and *Hercules* closer to the bow and begin exploring with a cable nearly as straight as a plumb line. Jim Newman and his crew also adjusted *Hercules*'s trim by removing 50 pounds from its lead weights to improve handling on the ocean floor.

By 4:20 p.m. we had the *Ron Brown* in a launch position and got the vehicles wet again. The cameras worked fine all the way to the bottom. Their lights caught the drifting, organic flecks of sea snow, making the ocean look like the interior of a gently shaken Christmas globe. *Argus* and *Herc* reached the bottom a few feet apart and a little less than a hundred feet from *Titanic*'s bow. The vehicles' trim seemed right as they hovered near the wreckage just beyond their vision. I ordered a move forward for *Hercules* that would put it under *Argus*'s lights.

I started to swear, then caught myself.

"We just lost *Hercules*," I said.

The signal from the ROV's high-definition camera had flickered, then gone out. But the camera wasn't the only thing that had failed.

"*Herc*'s black. No sonar, no nothing," came the report from the front of the control van. All telemetry had disappeared.

"I think you've got a dead vehicle," I said.

Hercules rocked as if comatose in the current, unable to use its thrusters to swim to *Titanic* or to the surface. It couldn't make even the most simple maneuvers as we hauled it in behind the *Ron Brown*'s stern. We would have to recover it "dead stick."

I ordered the crew to put a constant tension on the ROV's tether as we hauled it up. The resistance to being pulled, like a kite tugging at the end of a string, would give us a small measure of control as we

DAMAGE *from submersible impacts on the deck near the forward mast appears as yellow-orange wounds.*

tried to bring the vehicle on deck. Unfortunately, it would punish the tether. Fiber-optic cable isn't rope.

What had happened? Could the problem be fixed? The ascent began in silence.

Despite the complications of recovery without power, we got the vehicles safely aboard. Repair work began immediately, aided by clear sunlight.

For a diagnosis, Dave Wright, our laid-back fiber-optics mechanic, went straight to the tether that connected *Hercules* and *Argus*. It had a noticeable kink. Inside its yellow sheath, optical filaments probably had broken. For the tether to work properly, at least two of the three fibers had to function. However, when Dave shined a light into the fibers at one end of the tether, only one of the three passed it through to the other end. The other two were beyond repair.

Our team of engineers and mechanics spent the morning putting a new tether in place—our second of three on board—and adding strength to its ends with rubber tubing and a macramé of cords that Bruce Cowden, the ship's boatswain, had woven. He called it a Chinese finger puzzle, because the more the tether

TEAMWORK *strengthens* Hercules's *tether before a dive on June 1. Helping me are Jim Newman, top; Bruce Cowden, in gray cap; and Mark DeRoche, at left.*

yanked against *Herc* or *Argus*, the tighter the weave.

Finally, Dave polished the cable connectors and aligned the embedded optical fibers. There had been a noticeable loss of signal strength during the two dives, which had compromised *Herc*'s data even at the best of times. Dave's handiwork required precision and patience, as the channel of light carrying the video signals measured less than one-millionth of a meter wide. Slowly, calmly, he aligned and tested the filaments. They checked out OK.

"We are going to constantly push the envelope," I told our science crew by way of encouragement. "The images from the first dive were good, but we're going to beat that. Failure is not an option." We had not come so far to be bested by a broken fiber thinner than a human hair. The repair work done, we ran a final test on the signals from *Hercules*. Everything appeared normal on the video screens in the control van. At noon, we put our fish back in the water.

This time, we dropped them to the bottom in just over three hours, a faster descent than the two before. They arrived much nearer the wreckage, just as we planned. The *Ron Brown* pulled *Argus* over the bow section. The movement seemed perfect for giving *Hercules* its lead. "We're getting sweeter and sweeter on *Argus's* position, Bob," said navigator Jeremy Weirich, a NOAA lieutenant assisting us in the control van. Perhaps the third dive would be the charm.

We moved the vehicles around *Titanic's* port side and up toward the opening where the second funnel had stood. All the stacks had vanished, leaving only gaping holes. Rusticles covered the torn portions of the ship's steel like strands of a dirty mop. We came once again to the davit for Lifeboat No. 8 and got a closer look. The deck near the davit had collapsed.

"I would like to go 15 meters east," I told the pilots. "We're trying to get *Argus* in the center line of the ship so we can work both sides. "

OVER THE NEXT 12 hours, we finally got a long, slow look at *Titanic's* broken bow. *Hercules*, free and responsive compared with its first dive, hovered without restraint as the control-van pilots kept its tether loose during the early part of the dive.

The once-majestic mast sagged—plundered, stripped, and sad. When I last saw it in 1986, it had a beautiful brass light. That light was gone, as was nearly every other external feature on the mast's collapsed and broken length. In their place sat a crab,

nature's ornament, to replace those taken by the hands of man. Someday, in an ideal world, I would love to put the bell and light back on the mast, where they belong. That would be quite satisfying.

Up above, near where the fallen mast once had rested on the bridge, sat the cockeyed brass telemotor, which had held the wheel spun in desperation by Quartermaster Robert Hitchens. Now it had lost all wooden parts and stood naked and alone, leaning to port like a drunken sailor. Its rudder angle indicator, a metal arrow, was twisted toward the port side.

Had someone tried to remove the telemotor itself, or perhaps smashed into it accidentally? One piece of evidence gave mute testimony. A hole yawned under the bolts on the port edge of its brass base, as if someone had yanked or bumped it and torn the deck. "There are two options in life," I told the control-van crew as we examined the damage. "Laugh or cry."

Five plaques left by visitors since 1987 had been deposited in a line in front of the telemotor. I asked the camera operators to zoom in and focus on them one by one, starting with the most legible, at the far left. The metal plaque commemorated the Irish victims of the sinking who had boarded *Titanic* in Queenstown, now called Cobh. It was dated August 2000.

A second plaque paid tribute to the five postal workers who died on *Titanic*, while a third honored the late submersible expert Frank Busby.

The final two plaques had been laid by the British Titanic Society and the IMAX film crew that visited in 1991. Behind and to the right of the telemotor, a tiny American flag and artificial flowers had been laid down as a sort of makeshift memorial.

We moved *Herc* forward to examine the deck. Capstans gleamed in the lights, free of rusticles and decay. The current had polished them like mirrors. On one of the starboard capstans, the Explorers Club plaque I left in 1986 remained rightside up.

The forecastle drew gasps from our shipboard onlookers as *Hercules* flew gracefully above the center of *Titanic*. As often as our crew had seen it in photographs and paintings, nothing could compare with experiencing it in its entirety and in real time.

If seeing is believing, then witnessing such a legendary expanse of steel beneath the *Ron Brown* erased any doubts that remotely operated vehicles could do all that submersibles could do, and more. Our *Hercules*, like the mythological Greek hero who completed 12 seemingly impossible labors, had succeeded beyond the power of imagination. ■

WINDLASSES, *foreground, still are wound with Titanic's massive anchor chains. This view, taken during Hercules's first pass over the bow, is from above the forecastle, looking toward the prow.*

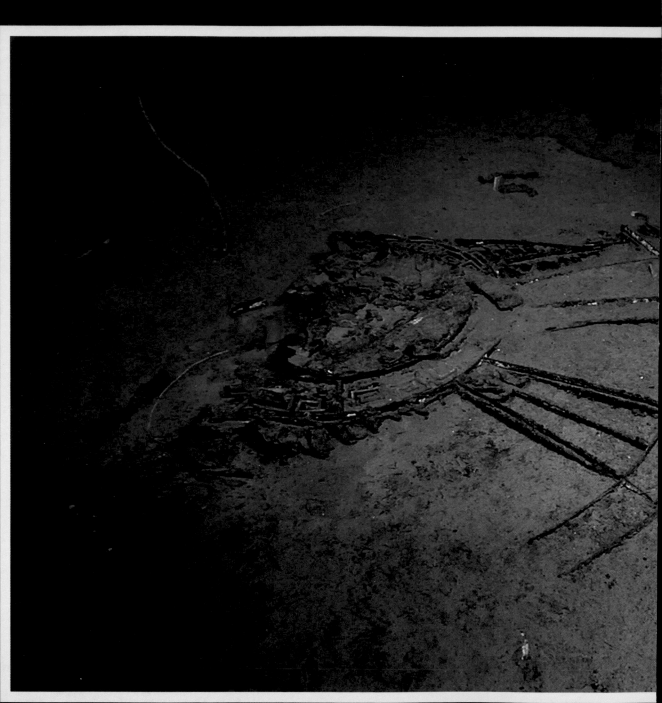

THE STERN

If Titanic's *bow represents grace, its stern speaks of death and destruction. After splitting from the bow, the stern imploded as it sank and struck the ocean floor at high speed, mangling decks and scattering debris like pellets from a shotgun. The skylight frame from one of the staircases, left, broke free and now rests in the mud of the debris field. Above, the grim graveyard has been invaded by nature and humanity. A tiny crustacean scuttles near a plastic cup dropped from the surface.*

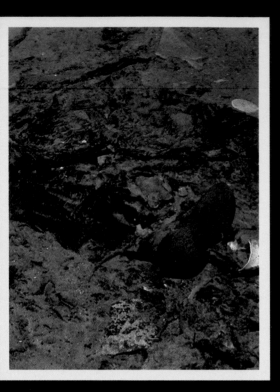

MORE THAN *1,000 bodies went to the bottom of the North Atlantic with the remains of* Titanic. *A slicker and heavy-duty boot situated just below its hem, above, fire the imagination: Could they have been on a body that landed near the stern and dissolved in the decades since the sinking?*

TWISTED METAL *testifies to the stern's agony, right. Deck plates flapped loose and crumpled, but two storage boxes, foreground, remained relatively intact. Ironically, destruction may have preserved the stern. Submarines don't land on this ghostly, jumbled junkyard.*

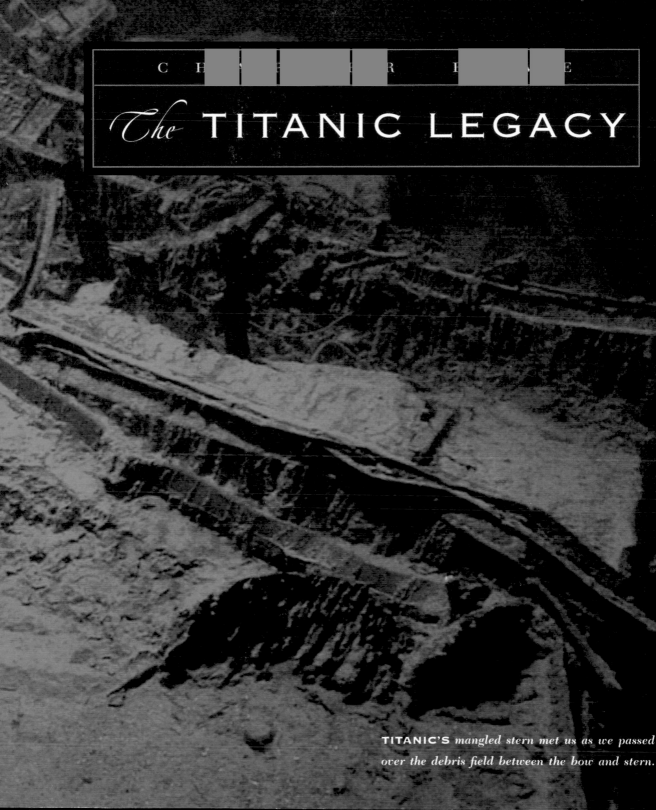

CHAPTER FIVE

The TITANIC LEGACY

TITANIC'S *mangled stern met us as we passed over the debris field between the bow and stern*

THE ROV HERCULES glided past a boom and slid along *Titanic's* fallen mast and anchor chains, connected by a cable to the *Ron Brown,* on the surface. *Herc's* cameras followed up the mast and across the well deck. The tether grew tight as we reached the doorway where, in 1912, Frederick Fleet and Reginald Lee emerged from the mast's internal staircase to begin their watch on the ship's last night afloat. Their crow's nest vanished years ago.

Next the pilot steered *Hercules* out in front of the ship and made it pirouette 180 degrees to face *Titanic* head on and to capture photographs of the bow. One was the "Leonardo DiCaprio shot" we had all talked about—a look at *Titanic's* forward-most point, where the rails come together forming a gentle V. Rusticles draped over the top rail and flowed along the prow like melted candle wax.

A pale crinoid, or sea lily, looking a little like a badminton shuttlecock, thrust its food-gathering arms out from a starboard rail.

We got a perfect shot of the ship's knife-edge. The sea snow rustled as the current picked up, but *Hercules* had no trouble focusing on the prow and the giant anchors just above the mud. Yes, *Titanic* was huge—*Herc's* lights revealed the top of its 60-foot hull. The rest was buried in the mud, but graceful, like a lithe athlete wrapped in a bedsheet.

"Welcome to Hollywood!" exclaimed Justin Manley, sitting in the navigator's seat in a corner of the van. He reached up and pointed at the prow as

THE AUXILIARY ANCHOR *lies on* Titanic's *forecastle, just below a rusticle-draped boom. Hercules's pilot had to watch the tether closely while moving around the prow, to keep free of the crane.*

it dominated the video screen before fading into the gloom. Score another point for telepresence.

Our tour took us close to the port rail, reminding me of a similar run I had made in 1986. Below the third porthole, *Hercules's* cameras zoomed in for a close look. Was the "T" still there? We strained our eyes for the first of the seven capital letters that spelled the ship's name but could see nothing amid the rusticles. "Let's get in real close and just sort of gape at it," I told the pilots.

But we still saw no evidence of the name *"Titanic."* What we did see, however, told us we were not the first to explore this spot. Amid the old-growth rusticles, ovals of new growth and nearly bare metal stood out. Their shape suggested that submersibles had nosed the side of the ship as deep-sea passengers had attempted to peer through the portholes and into the interior gloom. Further inspection revealed a recent gash across the port bow. It had sliced across one of the portholes and dislodged a curtain of rusticles.

As we continued to explore and photograph the forecastle, bridge, and boat deck, we found similar marks amid the green patina that covered the ship. The decks' wooden surface had long ago been eaten away, leaving only shells and apparently inedible caulking. At some spots the caulk had been crushed flat. These had to be footprints of submersibles that had parked on *Titanic*. One popular site seemed to be a clear landing spot next to the Grand Staircase opening. In the narrower spaces

that mini-subs could not hope to penetrate, the decks looked as they had in 1986. A growing list of evidence supported my suspicions about visitors.

Compared with our ROV, manned submersibles are large and clumsy. Some weigh 20 to 30 tons. When they bump into something, they do heavy damage. And because they do not have the dexterity of our underwater vehicles, they have to settle their carcasses to do their work. Their landing spots stood out like beacons. Holes, bent metal, sagging walls, and those yellowish footprints told the tale.

Sadly, the damage seemed most apparent on the boat deck aft of where the wheelhouse once stood. Capt. E. J. Smith's forward starboard sitting room had deteriorated considerably since my last visit. The outer walls had collapsed, leaving Smith's bathroom wide open. A pile of fallen rusticles filled his bathtub, its white porcelain gleaming. Taps for hot and cold water stood out brightly. Their pipes trailed aft.

It is not hard to imagine Smith washing his face here in his marble sink late on the night of April 14, 1912. Feeling the iceberg's impact, he rushed the few yards to the bridge to ask his first officer, William Murdoch, what had happened. Then he ordered a complete stop. Smith, Murdoch, and Fourth Officer Joseph Boxhall stepped into the now-vanished starboard bridge wing to look for the iceberg. Then Smith sent Boxhall to inspect the damage. Chief Officer Henry Wilde appeared and asked if the damage was serious. Smith, having just

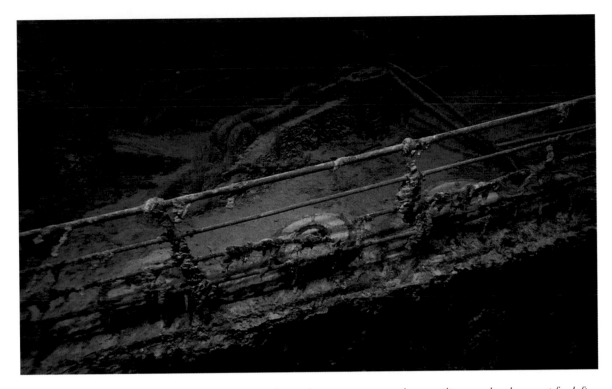

PORT BOW RAIL *screens rollers for mooring lines, chains, at center, and an auxiliary anchor boom, at far left.*

received the speedy Boxhall's report of water rising in the mail hold, said, "It is more than serious."

Wilde's actions that night remain a mystery. Survivors heard Smith tell him at 12:05 a.m. to uncover the lifeboats. Otherwise, the chief officer seldom appears in their accounts, and when he does, he takes little initiative. Added to the crew at Smith's request, Wilde boarded the ship shortly before it sailed. He may have been overwhelmed or felt out of place. Now, 92 years later, his cabin has begun to suffer the same fate as Smith's, its roof and walls buckling as if mashed by a giant fist. We

could not be sure during our initial inspection, but it appeared as if Wilde's quarters had suffered recent impact damage, possibly from a submersible swinging around the boat deck and clipping exterior walls.

Evidence of damage to *Titanic* deserved scientific documentation. We moved *Hercules* above the bow to create our crucial mosaic. A flash like lightning on a summer night illuminated the bow: Dwight Coleman had captured our first digital still photo of *Titanic*, soon to be followed by hundreds. The ROV's downward-looking digital cameras could

be programmed to fire every few seconds, or an operator in the control van could trip the flash and shutter manually. Either way, we planned to get plenty of images for the high-tech quilt we were about to stitch.

We locked *Hercules* into an automatic pattern to photograph the bow section. The Doppler Velocity Log navigation system moved *Herc* precisely on a rectangular grid, cameras snapping at each stop. *Hercules* performed like a Swiss watch, but *Argus* decided to act up. Its video camera had refused to tilt during an early swing over the bow and stayed locked up for the rest of the dive. That reduced *Argus's* roles to lighting the way for *Herc* and relaying digital photos to the surface.

Hercules began "mowing the lawn" in precise, square turns. The computer program designed to keep it at a constant altitude above *Titanic* got confused only when part of *Herc* hovered above the deck and part hung over the abyss. We decided to fix that problem by manually driving *Hercules* along the ship's outlines to snap mosaic photos, then combine those with the photography taken automatically—sort of like hand-drawing a doodle, then coloring it in with long, straight strokes.

Hercules and *Argus* got down to work in earnest. After two abbreviated dives, our two-vehicle

PRIVATE NO MORE, *Capt. E. J. Smith's bathroom has lost its outer wall. Pipes to the left of the bathtub, center, provided hot and cold water, both fresh and salt.*

exploration system was doing what it had been designed to do: Stay below for hours on end, executing task after task. "We can stand tall already," I told the crew in the control van as we began to document the bow section inch by inch. "And we've got a week to go."

Did the spirit of the sea hear me and laugh? This dive, while much longer than the first two, also ended sooner than we wanted. The weather forecast suggested a turn for the worse, with winds up to 30 knots and waves up to eight feet.

Then *Hercules* began to have problems. First one light went out. Then, as it attempted to pick up a six-year-old rusticle experiment station from the boat deck, its mechanical arm started hiccupping and bucking as if it had a demonic mind of its own. Finally, after about 20 frustrating minutes, pilot Todd Gregory got *Herc* to grab the experiment and drop it in the bio box. *Hercules* demonstrated its thrusters' fine motor skills by never touching the ship as it retrieved the experiment.

I went to bed around 1:30 a.m. that night but slept only three hours. Three decks down, in the control van, crew members on the early-morning watch had been keeping an eye on the weather. As the barometer fell, they decided they ought to pull the vehicles out. They had managed to mosaic the forepeak and portions of the top deck, completing a sweep of about one-third of the bow section. *Herc* and *Argus* broke the ocean surface at 6:45 a.m. on Wednesday, June 2.

For once, the forecasts were totally accurate. The vehicles emerged in eight-foot seas. Screaming winds blew a steady 30 knots, gusting up to 35, near gale force. Tom Orvosh, who had made the fiber-optic tethers, said it was the worst recovery he had ever seen.

The tether jerked taut as the crew maneuvered the vehicles behind the heaving stern. Fortunately, neither *Herc* nor *Argus* collided with the *Ron Brown*, but they did not escape unscathed. The up-and-down jerking of *Argus*'s cable caused severe damage to the mechanical termination where it attached to the sled. Welds in the aluminum braces at both ends of *Hercules*'s tether cracked, threatening *Herc* with a one-way trip to the bottom of the North Atlantic. And the mechanical arm continued to act crazily. All three problems would have to be fixed, and quickly. The live National Geographic Channel broadcast was only five days away.

Dave Wright said the towed sled had yanked out the end of its cable about an inch, and *Argus* and *Herc* could drop to the ocean floor if it was not repaired. He and the senior engineers reassembled the mechanical termination, then pull-tested 18,000 pounds from the *Ron Brown*'s stern.

The cracked aluminum welds aboard *Hercules* and *Argus* proved a tougher puzzle. They could not be welded back because of their proximity to the sensitive tether, whose embedded glass filaments would be destroyed by the heat of a torch. The cracked parts would have to be fixed some other way.

Acting Chief Engineer Jim Gatlin suggested that the aluminum be fitted with a support collar of steel that enfolded the broken part. The ship had plenty of scrap steel, and a band saw and arc welder to shape it. Brennan Phillips, a University of Rhode Island engineering graduate student, and ship's First Assistant Engineer Keegan Plaskon welded the end of a short steel pipe to a steel plate and sliced through the pipe lengthwise. The finished product looked like two halves of an ankle-high tee-ball stand. *Hercules* and *Argus* wore their

new steel collars later that day. A hydraulic cylinder in *Herc*'s mechanical arm was also replaced.

The weather stayed ugly that night, but the morning of Thursday, June 3, brought flatter seas and sunshine. It looked as if the vehicles would be ready to go over the side after lunch. We prepared for our fourth dive, which would be the first to the shattered stern, about a half mile south of the bow.

As the repair team checked and rechecked the vehicles, I attended to other chores such as the seemingly endless string of media communiqués

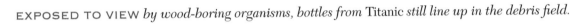

EXPOSED TO VIEW *by wood-boring organisms, bottles from* Titanic *still line up in the debris field.*

HERC'S ROBOTIC ARM *deposits a rusticle experiment station and retrieves an older one, center, near the bow.*

requested of me. The pace would only pick up once we had conducted our satellite press conference and started live Immersion and JASON webcasts. In one of my first interviews I chatted with Steve Inskeep of National Public Radio. He asked about the damage and decay to *Titanic* and the ship's continuing allure. Then he threw me a curve. "I wonder if there have occasionally been moments when you almost wished you hadn't done it?" Inskeep asked, referring to our discovery in 1985.

"No," I answered truthfully. Then I realized that this was an opportunity to get millions of Americans to consider important issues. With *Titanic*, I could

get them thinking about the greater world of ocean exploration and make a pitch for multinational preservation protocols, to protect not just *Titanic* but all shipwrecks in international waters.

"The *Titanic* is critical because people are fascinated by it, and will listen to the call to preserve it," I said. "But ancient antiquities is my great interest. We think the deep sea is a giant museum. We've been finding shipwrecks dating back to the Phoenicians, the Romans, the Greeks—and those ships are at peril. It's the Wild West out here. There are no laws governing much of antiquity in the deep sea. . . . We can use *Titanic* as a platform to present our case that the deep sea is the biggest museum of the world. It has more artifacts in it than all the museums of the world combined, and yet there's no lock on the door. We need to generate international laws to protect human antiquity."

ARGUS AND HERCULES went under at noon. Then I had another round of interviews. I chatted with dozens of journalists, mostly print reporters, by conference call as I watched the vehicles descend.

I likened *Titanic* to a grand lady in her grave whose jewelry has been removed. The ship and its debris field had been picked over by submersibles seeking artifacts, I told the reporters, and the ship has suffered a series of dents and dings. I had not seen as much biological decay as I had been led to expect, I told them. The forward part of the bow still looked regal, as it had in 1986. Rusticles, while voracious, didn't appear to be as dangerous as clumsy submersibles. I called for a protocol that would prevent landings and collisions with *Titanic*, but I stopped short of advocating a ban on visits. If people wish to see the ship for themselves, that's OK, I said, but they must learn to respect it.

There was more at stake in preserving *Titanic* than the fate of just one ship, I explained. By documenting what has happened to *Titanic*, my science team hoped not only to build support for preservation but also to begin to formulate a strategy to counter its deterioration. The knowledge gained through the study of *Titanic* will guide future archaeologists, and the protection afforded this shipwreck could be a model for others. "As the *Titanic* goes, so goes human history beneath the sea," I concluded.

Amid all this activity, microbiologist Roy Cullimore was examining his beloved rusticles. Gray-haired and bearded, with a penchant for blue jeans and zip-up sweatshirts, Roy is the world's expert on the complex microbial communities of rusticles. He has even managed to grow them in his office in Saskatchewan. He delights in discussing microbial activity taking place everywhere—in our planet's waters, throughout its atmosphere, and, of course, on *Titanic*.

It was Roy's experiment that *Herc* had just collected. Roy had placed the array of steel bars on *Titanic*'s bow in 1998. During our voyage, Roy would retrieve one other platform, placed in the same year, and leave two new ones beside the ship. The rusticle platforms he retrieved would be stripped, X-rayed, and analyzed at Roy's company in Canada to determine how much iron the rusticles had consumed. The findings would give us a rate that we could apply to the ship as a whole.

Rusticles are like living, porous concrete. The microbes create living quarters with techniques like those by which humans make synthetic stone. They start with threadlike polymer structures and then crystallize iron, calcium, and a bit of

C reating a photomosaic of *Titanic* was so much easier the second time around. In 1985, *Knorr* dragged our towed sled *ANGUS* across *Titanic's* bow section dozens of times at a height of about 25 feet. With each pass, at intervals of seven seconds, images were made by three automated, still-frame Benthos film cameras attached to the sled.

They could not immediately know what the film had captured. *ANGUS* possessed no real-time video, so they could only guess when the sled had moved above its target. Its cameras continued making images every seven seconds. Only later, when the 50-foot rolls of film coiled in each of the tubelike cameras had been developed did they know whether they had good pictures of the ship. It was kind of like tossing darts at a board tacked up in a darkened room, then turning on the lights to figure the score.

All told, the photographers shot more than 70,000 stills. Of those, months later, 108 images formed the monochrome mosaic that appeared in a 1987 issue of NATIONAL GEOGRAPHIC magazine. Two graph-

THE MOSAICS

ics specialists worked in collaboration with the magazine and Madison Press Books, painstakingly matching up the photographs and adjusting variations in perspective, angle, and depth. Despite so many photos, three small sections of the bow eluded the cameras. A video image filled one of the slots in the final mosaic, and dashed lines indicated the other two.

Flash forward to 2004. Our remotely operated vehicle *Hercules* carried two PixelFly high-performance digital imaging systems mounted to focus downward from a metal frame. The ROV also had a Doppler Velocity Log navigation system, DVL-nav for short, that could figure *Hercules's* position precisely, lock it into a grid in three-dimensional space, and drive it along a programmed course. When *Herc* "mowed the lawn" above *Titanic,* it moved in perfectly straight lines, stopping every few seconds to snap a digital image. No need to process any film: Within minutes, the images were in our computers aboard the *Ronald H. Brown.*

As we explored *Titanic* and worked on the mosaic, we referred to a blown-up copy of the original mosaic, stuck on the side wall of our control van on the *Ron Brown's* stern. Mosaicking began with the

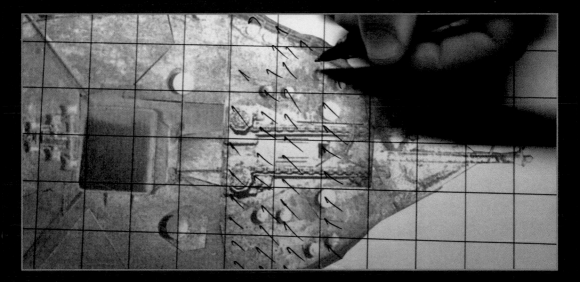

anchor windlasses and chains, one of the more visually stunning parts of *Titanic*'s bow. We used check marks, shown above, to indicate where *Hercules* had snapped a digital image. Adjacent images needed significant overlap for proper merging in the final mosaic.

When our vehicles had mechanical difficulties, we supplemented our collection of images with digital frames taken from *Hercules*'s high-definition video cameras. A data logger in the control van manually captured images while watching the 52-inch video monitor. In this way we were able to generate the first-ever mosaic of *Titanic*'s stern section.

The PixelFly stills and captured video frames totaled thousands of images. Using sophisticated software to compensate for a range of angles, shadows, and other variables, Hanumant Singh at the Woods Hole Oceanographic Institution manipulated the digital images on a computer. Common elements in successive photos were aligned to create a seamless color mosaic. This time the process took weeks instead of months.

The photomosaics act as baselines for comparison. By examining the 2004 mosaic of the bow section next to the same mosaic created from 1985 photographs, we can quickly see where *Titanic* has declined since my first visits. Surely this most recent photographic exercise will not be the last, and future photomosaics will chart the changes from what our cameras captured in 2004—and so on. As a scientist, I appreciate the way these photographic documents freeze concrete images of *Titanic* at specific points in time. They provide crucial data for those who wish to preserve the great ship: objective, precise observations instead of rumor and anecdote.

The fact that the mosaics are beautiful artwork in their own right is a bonus.

aluminum. The outer wall of rusticles is heavy with iron, which protects the resident colonies of bacteria and mold. Rusticle skin grows tougher and darker with age, which makes it easy to spot new ones.

Young rusticles extract iron from a source like the *Titanic*'s hull. As they grow, they incorporate more and more of the metal into their communal structure. If the rusticles stop consuming, they die, but if they keep adding iron, they become so heavy they break off—and then die. They fall away and leave a gap that encourages new rusticles to form. It's a circle of life.

Rusticles cover nearly the entire exterior surface of *Titanic*. Inside, they're even thicker. If you peer inside the portholes on the starboard side of the lower promenade deck, you'll probably see rusticles pressed up against the glass. In some places, the interior seems a forest of red stalactites in a darkened cave.

Our study of *Titanic*'s rusticles should not only give us a possible timeline for the ship's future decay, but also teach us more about how rusticles work. That should help us learn how to stop their voracious appetite for destruction or, by the same token, how to encourage rusticle growth for beneficial purposes. Roy envisions one possible use: Rusticles could be grown on underwater oil rig platforms once they have finished pumping.

Roy believes that rusticle consumption of *Titanic*'s iron has accelerated in the last eight years. He is collecting hard data to be sure. Just looking at the ship, I have the sense that the rusticles have grown faster at the stern. Two reasons come to mind. First, about 24 tons of food was stored in the stern. When the ship hit the ocean floor, that organic material gave the microorganisms a head start on growth. Second, rusticles prefer a torn surface to a smooth one. The crashed stern offered plenty of footholds. Today, most of the stern's rusticles are old and brown in comparison to the bow section's crop, which looks younger, brighter, and more active. Of course, submersible contact may have knocked old growth away and made room for new.

Just how active are the rusticles? Roy put an experiment station next to the bow on one of our early dives of 2004. Four days later, when *Hercules* returned to the site, the iron in a sample of rolled steel—not used in shipbuilding today, but common in 1912—already had a light coating of rusticle microorganisms. So had bits of welding.

Roy's observations also confirm that *Titanic* is sagging. There seems to be a continuing collapse on the upper promenade and boat deck. It is difficult to say how much of the collapse is due to biological decay, how much to human abuse. We will have to analyze our photographs before drawing conclusions. As I told the journalists, I found the rumors of "rapid decay" to be exaggerated.

Hercules and *Argus* reached *Titanic*'s stern shortly after 3 p.m. "It took us a while to realize it," Jim said of the pinpoint accuracy of this dive. "It's all a jumble down there." True enough, the stern is not as aesthetically pleasing as the bow. *Hercules's*

AS IF APPLIED *with a palette knife, rusticles cling to a window frame like blobs of orange and ochre paint.*

and *Argus*'s pilots worked the vehicles into the best arrangement for lighting. We gazed at the monitors and examined the deck plates, which had peeled back and shattered on impact. The mess did not suggest a ship so much as a junkyard. Examining *Titanic* by scrutinizing the stern would be like trying to understand what the World Trade Center once looked like by studying the post-9/11 rubble.

"Do your classic pirouette, Todd," I said. A well-rehearsed spin panned *Hercules*'s cameras across the stern, bathed in light from *Argus* about 40 feet overhead. We were near the end of the ship. Section plates on the starboard side had been

blown out. Two electric cranes on the ruptured poop deck tilted at a 45-degree angle. The stern's implosion, then impact on the bottom, explained the crazy-world scrapyard before us.

Lights from *Argus* turned the deck as bright as morning. Thrusters pushed *Hercules* toward one of the crane's levers and electrical box. *Herc*'s camera brought out the heads of individual bolts and brass letters that spelled out "Hoisting Clutch," "Lowering," "Emergency." Nearby, a sky-blue lobster perched on the crane's foundation. A feathery coral waved in the current. If we had wanted to, we could have counted the threads on the exposed bolts. The clarity boggled the mind. The ocean water seemed as clear as glass; the cameras picked out every detail. "Nicely done, gentlemen," I said.

We wandered about, stopping to examine anything interesting in our path. A chamber pot, a third-class spittoon, a huge engine-room wrench, and a brass furnace register came into view. We continued toward the fantail, carefully avoiding overhanging cables and debris. The appearance of huge fairlead rollers, used in guiding the ship's

mooring lines, signaled that we had reached the edge, where I left the plaque in 1986 in tribute to *Titanic* historian Bill Tantum and *Titanic*'s victims. The only plaque we could see had been placed by filmmaker James Cameron. We zoomed in on his words: "The 1,500 souls lost here still speak, reminding us always that the unthinkable can happen, but for our vigilance, humility and compassion."

There are times I feel like a scientist during these dives, working as an objective professional to

A TORN SECTION *of* Titanic's *hull, with one glass porthole intact, lies in the debris field near the stern.*

make sure every technical operation is carried to completion. And then there are times that I feel overwhelmed by the surroundings, and I just have to soak in the emotion of the moment. This was one of those times. I ordered the vehicles to hover for a bit so we could drink in the view of the stern.

"That's the diving board of death," I whispered. Hundreds of people who failed to get into one of the lifeboats moved toward the stern as *Titanic* slowly sank at the bow. They clambered away from the icy water and up the sloping decks. Frightened passengers, mostly from third class, prayed fervently, received absolution from Father Thomas Byles, and, in their final moments, jumped or plunged into the water. Most died of exposure before they had a chance to drown.

We compared our view of the stern with the paintings Ken Marschall completed nearly two decades ago. They were virtually identical: a mass of twisted metal. The condition of this portion of the ship made it a nearly impossible landing for a submersible.

Hercules and *Argus* dropped back, and the ROV descended toward the ocean floor. I had

A SPITTOON *in the debris field testifies to* Titanic's *human element. Brass objects and artifacts made from other nonferrous metals have defied the passage of time.*

hoped to see the propeller and the rudder, but the quarters were too cramped by overhanging rusticles. We could clearly see the single track left by *Alvin* as it daringly sneaked under the stern 18 years earlier.

We backed away to get more freedom of movement. Scattered debris near the stern stretched before us, a yard sale of artifacts. More bedsprings. A ceramic container that might have been a shaving mug. A perfect stack of serving plates, their metal turned green. It was interesting that they had not scattered on impact. Perhaps they had rested in a wooden cabinet that disappeared over the years.

At 8 p.m., we left the stern for a tour of the debris field that extended toward the bow. As we had discovered on our initial dive, much of the field had been cleaned out, leaving submersible skid marks and muddy mounds. Still, there was enough here to suggest the mountain of material that burst from *Titanic* as it split apart. Another boiler, one of 29 that fed steam to the ship's reciprocating engines and low-pressure turbine, appeared on the floor. How many boilers had spilled from the ship, and how many remained inside, we could not be sure. Now a feathery red coral and green lichenlike growth adorned this boiler's black iron. We gasped at a white circle on top of the boiler, thinking it might be a teacup like one we found in 1986. It turned out to be a crab.

We found a silver serving dish, also turned green. A brass faucet was stuck in the mud, its spigot pointing upward, its metal polished clean by the current. Nearby lay a brick that once insulated a boiler's lining. And farther on, a teapot with its lid open and a white cup decorated with the image of a red flag rested on the bottom. *Hercules* turned, and we could see the White Star label opposite the cup handle. Sea snow falling for millennia created the deep, soft sediment of the North Atlantic, but it barely dusted the cup: a graphic reminder that it's an old Earth, but a relatively young *Titanic*.

The watch crew changed at midnight. Soon they debated whether to bring the vehicles back to the surface. *Argus* had been giving us fits with its sonar transponder. The control crew had no way of knowing *Argus*'s position except by looking at *Herc*'s butt cam monitor. *Hercules* added to the troubles when its mechanical arm turned screwball again, as engineer Brennan Phillips put it. It flailed and smacked the frame that held the mosaicking cameras, knocking them 90 degrees so they pointed at *Herc* instead of down. The cameras were not damaged, but we could not do any mosaicking with

them until we hauled up the ROV and manually repositioned them.

Even both problems together might not have tipped the debate, but a new forecast called for rain and high seas on Friday morning. We decided to retrieve the vehicles and get everything fixed. Rain began to slam the deck as engineers fixed the mechanical arm and installed a new camera frame. Meanwhile, the first of the live Immersion broadcasts got under way. ABC correspondent Jay Schadler and the video production team decided to shoot the interviews with our science specialists at the stern, right in front of *Hercules*. As Jay chatted with Craig and later with Jeremy, raindrops pummeled everyone on deck.

WHEN THE SKIES cleared and the vehicles were certified ready, we put them over the side for dive number five. It was the afternoon of Friday, June 4, and this time our destination was the wide-open debris field. The engineers smiled at the prospect of exploring without fear of *Hercules*'s tether catching on any cables, decks, davits, booms, or rusticles. They also looked forward to some surprises. Large portions of the bow and stern have become familiar through photographs, paintings, and repeated visits, but large sections of the debris field have never been explored. Although submersibles have removed many

DINING ROOM PLATTERS *in the debris field remain stacked as if their container disintegrated around them.*

artifacts, they haven't been everywhere, and they haven't gotten everything. The three watch crews agreed on an informal competition to see who would be the first to find the shoes and boots I had declared a prime target.

We knew that *Hercules* had a better chance of finding artifacts than any submersible. It could hover and glide through swaths of ocean floor well lit by *Argus* overhead. It began to prowl the sediment between stern and bow and indeed did find much that the salvors had missed or deemed too ordinary to retrieve. A ripped piece of hull plating, its rivets long gone, leaving a line of holes like

eyelets in a tennis shoe. An upside-down porcelain toilet. Stacks of wine bottles, their corks pistoned inside by tremendous water pressure. The bottles often appeared in neat geometric patterns, indicating they had landed inside crates.

Herc found the same cast-iron deck chair frame that *Alvin* had photographed in 1986. It gave me a thrill to see it in exactly the same orientation as it had had 18 years ago—upright, facing our left, covered with a light greenish tint that made it look almost bronze. Oxidized iron deposits had encroached from across the ocean floor. In the original photograph, the orange carpet stopped a few inches from the frame. Now, it oozed beneath the seat and seemed to nip at the back legs.

We also saw the metallic frame for the glass dome of one of the ship's elegant staircases. In 2001 Cameron had sent his own ROVs inside *Titanic*. Finding nothing to suggest that the Grand Staircase had collapsed internally, he speculated that it may have broken free, pulled upward by its buoyant wood. A seaman had testified in 1912 that he had seen what looked like a floating staircase after the ship sank. The dome in the debris field does not prove that the staircase dislodged and floated free, but it does argue against an internal collapse.

A dark satchel had surrendered its sides to the corruption of the sea, but its edges remained intact and still held a hinge and a clasp. Had this belonged to a professional—a doctor, perhaps? I was strangely moved by this item that had once been important to someone who sailed on *Titanic*.

SEDIMENT, *not coffee or tea, covers the bottom of a White Star Line mug in the debris field.*

Evidence of recent human visitation—and human error—abounded. We saw plenty of submersible track marks. We found dive weights and a submersible's black thruster cowling amid the older debris.

Life also flourished in *Herc*'s headlights. An orange crab carrying a champagne-colored anemone scuttled by. The piggyback anemone's red tentacles swished in the crab's wake. Catalina Martinez, a biologist on the science team, said the pairing of the two animals is common. Crabs benefit from the camouflage and protection provided by the stinging tentacles, while the anemone gets to move.

Finally, before dawn on Sunday, June 6, while nearly everyone else slept, the bleary-eyed watch that had Tom piloting *Hercules*, Dave Wright on *Argus*, and Justin as navigator, found what I had so dearly wanted to see. Shoes.

In an apparently unexplored section of the debris field, shoes and boots began to show up in *Herc*'s field of vision. A single shoe came first, then pairs. High-buttoned shoes. Work boots. Delicate, feminine shoes.

I was in the van Sunday morning when we came upon three scenes that stood out among all the rest. An obvious pair of matched high-heeled shoes rested next to a couple of small, white dishes that looked as if they might have been souvenirs. The dishes were painted with the word "Stockholm."

A second boot thrust its sole toward the sky. Around it, scattered cups and saucers flashed white against the blacks and browns of the background. We looked closer and a dark shape above the boot took form: a slicker. A belt flopped to the right. A shape on top suggested a sleeve drawn diagonally across the front. The orientation of the boot and the garment fired our imagination. Perhaps one person was wearing both articles of clothing when the ship sank. There was no way to tell.

The third image was the most powerful of all.

"Is that a comb?" Jeremy asked, peering at the plasma screen directly in front of him.

"It is!" I said. "It's a comb. A woman's hair comb."

A decorative comb stood fixed in the mud, teeth pointing up. It rested atop a second comb, smaller and black. To the right, a third comb peeked from beneath metallic debris. In front of the large, upright comb rested a woman's shoes, heels in and toes out. Red-and-white floor tiles, the same kind photographed in a third-class cabin before *Titanic* sailed, lay scattered between and around the shoes.

We moved *Hercules* to a higher angle to shoot down on the shoes from the perspective of a standing human. Now a third shoe came into view to the right. Smaller, it belonged to a child or teenager. As we stared at this frozen scene, we recognized a shiny disk at the bottom of the screen as the remains of a hand mirror. Bits of its shiny backing glinted in the lights.

I shivered. Whether from the sight before me or from the particularly frigid air in the control van where I sat bundled in my coat, I could not be sure. We cannot stare at such evidence of human tragedy without grasping the fundamental truth of the *Titanic* wreckage: It is a graveyard, a repository for lost hopes and dreams. Is there anyone who would prefer seeing a simple comb in a museum display, to seeing it in the full context of drama and tragedy? This was a ship that once rang with hundreds of human voices. Now it was silent.

I was not the only one who felt moved by the events of the fifth dive. As *Hercules* and *Argus* still roamed the ocean floor, the Saturday night movie played in the ship's lounge: *A Night to Remember,* the 1953 film about the *Titanic* disaster. It packed the house. "Just think," somebody said in the darkness as an actor portraying one of the Marconi operators radioed *Titanic*'s final longitude and latitude. "We're at those same coordinates."

The fifth dive kept getting longer. At last, *Hercules* and *Argus* were showing their potential. The vehicles notched 24 hours, then 48, and even began a third day underwater. It was a welcome

PORTHOLE FRAME *rests beside chains and sandbags used by salvagers to weight containers for artifacts. These were left behind as the quarry was hauled to the surface.*

change from problems earlier in the week. Brennan joked that he had forgotten what the vehicles looked like. *Hercules* thoroughly explored the debris field and completed the mapping of the bow. Its cameras snapped more than 2,200 digital images in a complete survey. The expedition's primary objective was accomplished.

Every minute extended *Hercules*'s endurance record far beyond any previous dives. My plan was to leave the two vehicles underwater even longer, through the live broadcast on Monday night, then recover them and fix a nagging glitch in one of *Herc*'s cameras.

But that was not to be. *Herc* lost power on Monday morning, more than 60 hours into the dive. We had no choice but to recover the vehicles and hope they could be repaired in time for the broadcast.

When we hauled *Hercules* and *Argus* up, two problems became evident. First, one of *Herc*'s internal fiber-optic connections had failed. The link between the tether and the ROV's main bottle, a pressurized container for electronics, had to be replaced, although the bottle itself was unharmed. Second, the metal fibers at the end of the tow cable had begun to abrade. The mechanical termination had been designed to pitch up and down, but it could not easily support unexpected rolling, up-and-down movements.

That was a relatively easy fix, but it took a long time. A repair crew rebuilt the cable's end. Mechanics also tinkered with *Herc's* faulty connection and got a proper signal. But no sooner did *Hercules* splash into the waves than its signals to the control van went dead again. The deck crew parked the stricken ROV on the fantail for diagnosis. *Zap!* As soon as *Hercules* powered up, its tether smoked and sizzled.

It was Monday afternoon, just hours from the live broadcast. I knew it would not help *Hercules* for me to get anxious. You could feel the pressure in the air. The National Geographic Channel had promoted a live broadcast from *Titanic*, to begin at 9 p.m. If we were to get *Hercules* and *Argus* to the shipwreck before the broadcast, the vehicles would have to leave *Ron Brown* no later than 6 p.m., and

KNOB TO *a long-vanished door has wood fragments attached. Contact with metal can retard wood decay.*

even then there were no guarantees, given the unpredictability of ocean currents and a 2.5-mile cable. As if things weren't tough enough, the engineers decided that *Herc*'s entire tether had to be replaced. We had a backup on board that had served us well during the Black Sea expedition in 2003, but one of its three optical filaments was broken. Two would have to do. "Seconds count!" I exclaimed—as if I needed to remind these professionals that the clock was ticking.

I had no business being on the fantail, but I had to go there and lend a hand. The engineers from the Institute for Exploration and the University of Rhode Island were the absolute best experts to handle the kind of rapid and sensitive repair work we needed. My presence, I thought, would communicate a sense of urgency and commitment. I picked up a knife as a small crowd gathered to attach the new tether to *Herc*. Another group worked with *Argus.* In my haste, I cut my finger and baptized the final tether in blood.

PASSENGERS' *shoes lie beside tile, a hand mirror, and three combs: two for adornment, and one, by the mirror, which may have been used to part hair that final night.*

SEATING, *previous pages, now and then reveals Edwardian touches: a filigreed metal frame for a deck chair, left, the same one photographed during the 1986 expedition; and, right, elegant chairs in the upper promenade's Reading Room.*

PANIC GRIPS *those still on* Titanic's *boat deck in a scene from the film* A Night to Remember.

At least the weather decided to cooperate. The two vehicles hit the water at 5:20 p.m. on Monday, June 7, to start our sixth and final dive. The blue water and white bubbles that filled the video monitors, normally boring, now thrilled us.

Hercules could see.

HERC AND ARGUS reached the ocean bottom in two and a half hours, their fastest descent yet. Even more miraculously, Justin navigated them so they arrived less than 170 feet from the bow. By 9:15, about

a half-hour ahead of the time they were to be shown live at the end of the program, they were in position.

The program cut to us live and on schedule. Our resilient ROV sent its video feed to the world. In real time, viewers saw *Titanic* through the eyes of *Hercules* as it rose above the forecastle and slid down the main axis of the ship, dropped off the port side and followed the railings toward the prow. Bitts, capstans, and a fallen port rail, along with a mysterious yellow rod on the deck, appeared in the video monitor. As *Hercules* reached the front, Jim Newman, piloting *Argus*, started to caution *Herc* pilot Todd Gregory not to swing to starboard. The floating tether looked as if it might get caught on the overhanging boom. But as Jim watched, the buoyant yellow football lifted the tether as if by magic, clearing the danger. "Keep going!" Jim told Todd, who swung *Hercules* to the left to frame the leading edge of *Titanic*. *Herc* then rose along the forward boom, pulled back, and the legendary ship melted into the gloom. The best possible parting shot of *Titanic* had come off without a

The red-eyed watch crews alternated between yawns and goofy giddiness. *Hercules* came upon an unidentified bit of metal on the ocean floor, and the crew called it a "doo-lateral framistat."

We laid my replacement plaque near the bow and headed for the stern section again. We never did find the plaque I had left there in 1986, or the doll's head I had hoped to find—two of the very few disappointments of the voyage.

"THE DEEP SEA IS A MUSEUM THAT CONTAINS MORE HISTORY THAN ALL OF THE MUSEUMS OF THE WORLD COMBINED. YET THERE IS NO LAW COVERING THE VAST MAJORITY OF SHIPWRECKS, AND A GREAT DEAL IS AT RISK."

—ROBERT D. BALLARD, 2004

hitch, those final seconds totally impromptu.

"That was very nice," Jim said with a New Englander's typical understatement.

"Wow! Yes!" I shouted as soon as we were off the air. Cheers, applause, and hugs filled the control van. Even my wife, Barbara, a producer who feels no qualms about honestly assessing television quality, told me by phone that we had hit a home run. The final day at the site seemed anticlimactic. The adrenaline had drained from the control van.

Hercules and *Argus* spent Tuesday mosaicking back and forth across the tangled metal of the stern, one of our lower priorities for the voyage. *Herc* got a little closer to the rudder, but we could see none of the giant propellers. Threatened by overhanging tangles, we decided to pull away from the edge of the ship.

The barometer began falling. I ordered the vehicles out of the water for the last time at 2:35 p.m. on June 8. The last image in *Herc*'s cameras was

the top of a giant reciprocating engine, a studded
circular cap that looked like
the crown of a chessboard
queen. With that, we said
goodbye to *Titanic*.

One of my last tasks at
the site was to speak from
on board with representa-
tives of the G8 industrial-
ized nations meeting in
Georgia. I shared my vision
of *Titanic*'s future and
called for an international
effort to preserve the
museums of the ocean
floor. I endorsed the treaty signed by Britain in
2003. My biggest fear, I told the delegates, was that
the technology to reach the ocean floor had fallen
into private hands. Unregulated salvors could
recover artifacts before they had been properly
documented. "We really need international coop-
eration, and we need it now," I said.

Ask, and ye shall receive. The good news
reached me as I prepared for an Immersion Project
webcast: The U.S. Department of State had
decided to follow Britain's lead and sign the *Titanic*
protection treaty. Craig McLean, who had pur-
sued the treaty for a decade, came up and grabbed
my hand, butter-coated from our celebratory
dinner of crab legs. He gave me a vigorous

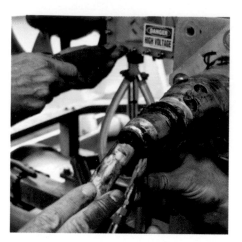

RACING AGAINST *time, the crew and
I install a new tether between* Hercules *and*
Argus *before a National Geographic Channel
broadcast. In my haste, I cut my finger.*

handshake along with his
congratulations.

If put into effect by
Congress, the treaty would
create a common protocol to
control access to *Titanic* and
could punish rule-breakers
who are citizens of the signing nations or whose ships
call at those nations' ports.
The State Department said
that the treaty designated
Titanic "as an international
maritime memorial, recog-
nizing the men, women and
children who perished and
whose remains should be given appropriate respect."
Parties to the treaty "will also protect the scientific,
cultural and historical significance of the wreck site
by regulating, within their jurisdiction, dives to the
Titanic shipwreck, including the hull, cargo and other
artifacts at the wreck site." The treaty would not ban
legal salvage operations. I later learned that RMS
Titanic Inc. said it would support the treaty if it agrees
with the final legislation.

These are steps in the right direction. France
and Canada also have taken part in the discussion
and, ideally, will sign the treaty, since Canada is the
closest landmass to the shipwreck and France has
the technology to reach it. So does Russia, so I hope
it signs, too.

I T WAS THE PERFECT END to a nearly perfect expedition. *Titanic* spoke, and our science team recorded that voice. It spoke to the officials in Washington who decided to protect it. It spoke to children all over America who followed our explorations and got to experience real-world math and science. It spoke to television viewers around the world who reveled in its enduring strength and beauty despite all it has suffered.

And it spoke to me.

As the *Ron Brown* turned west and got under way for Woods Hole, Massachusetts, I stood on the deck and threw my souvenir baseball cap labeled "Return to Titanic" over the side in a burst of emotion. I have plenty of others, I thought to myself. *Titanic* could have this one.

Will I come back? Who knows. Maybe in another 18 years. Given what we've seen on this voyage, as well as the good news about the treaty, *Titanic* probably will look much the same in two

HERCULES, *lighted by* Argus, *swings around the crane at* Titanic's *prow during the live broadcast.*

decades. I do look forward to fulfilling my own dream of turning *Titanic* into a museum, through the technological wizardry of telepresence. The way we shared *Titanic* with the world in 2004 was a great start, but it was only the beginning.

That night, the *Ron Brown* slammed into 50-knot winds and 20-foot seas. Waves pounded the bow like Thor's hammer and sent spray up higher than the bridge. The wind nearly imprisoned Scott Stamps in his communications control van on the bow. He could open the side door a crack, but knew if he let go it would fly open and never shut again. He had to call two people down from the bridge to brace the door so he could escape.

Nobody slept that night as the ship steered violently through the storm. We didn't care. We'd be coming into port in three days with a broom tied to our mast, signifying our clean sweep of tasks at the *Titanic*.

I knew there would be time for sleep in the days and weeks to come. For one thing, I felt assured that the great *Titanic* would also sleep soundly for a long, long time. Our efforts had shared its mystery, its sorrows, and its glory to the world—and we had done our part to see that the remains of the ship would rest unharmed, a monument to hope and history, on the floor of the North Atlantic where they belonged. ■

A TUNICATE, *primitive kin to vertebrates and termed for its leatherlike "tunic," sways at* Titanic's *bow. This animal attaches itself by a stalk and filters water for food.*

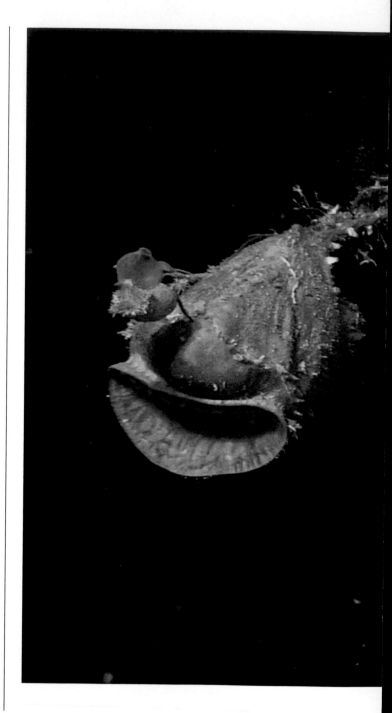

MOSAIC 1987: Titanic's *bow appeared in* NATIONAL GEOGRAPHIC's *October issue. From 70,000 stills taken by cameras on* ANGUS, *more than 100 plus one image captured from video were pieced together to create depth and perspective — a majestic portrait from crow's nest to the No. 3 funnel, at the break.*

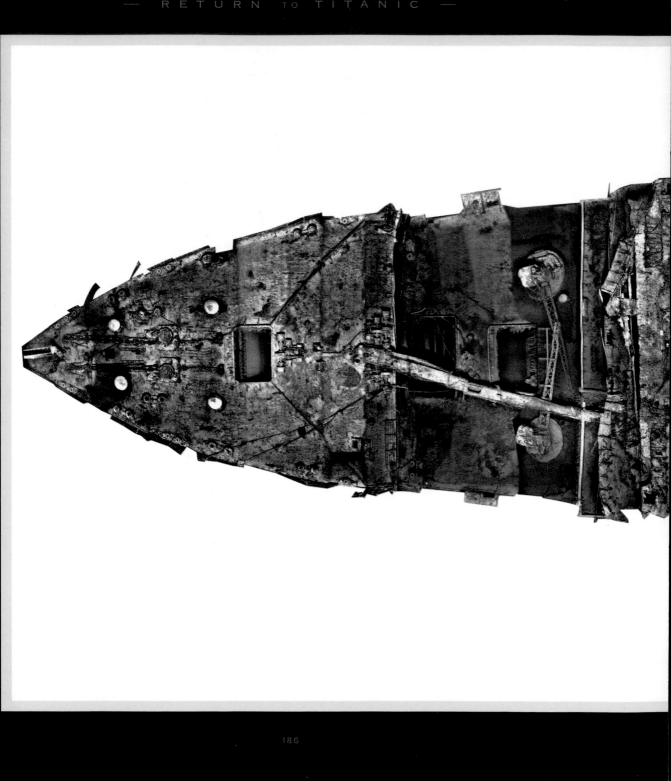

MOSAIC 2004: *Digital still and video cameras made thousands of images, then software combined them to show* Titanic *today: victim of natural deterioration and of salvagers, who have taken thousands of objects from her deck and debris field. Gone is the crow's nest, and sub tracks mar her hull.*

INDEX

DEDICATION

*To William Benjamin Aymar Ballard and Emily Rose
Penrhyn Ballard, my ten- and six-year-old children,
who already possess the hearts of explorers.*
—Robert D. Ballard

ILLUSTRATIONS CREDITS

Key: Institute for Archaeological Oceanography (IAO); Institute for Exploration (IFE);University of Rhode Island Grad. School of Oceanography (URI-GSO); Woods Hole Oceanographic Institution (WHOI).

Cover, IFE & IAO/URI-GSO; 1, IFE & IAO/URI-GSO; 2-3, IFE & IAO/URI-GSO; 4, Hulton-Deutsch Coll./CORBIS; 7, Time Life Pictures/Getty Images; 8-9, Ralph White/CORBIS; 10, Emory Kristof/WHOI; 11, Titanic Historical Society; 14, WHOI; 15, Christie's Images/CORBIS; 16, Bettmann/ CORBIS; 18, WHOI; 20-1, Emory Kristof; 23, CORBIS; 24, 25, Ralph White/CORBIS; 26-7, Hulton-Deutsch Coll./CORBIS; 28 (UP), Bettmann/CORBIS; 28 (LO), Ernest H. Mills/Getty Images; 29 (UP), Bettmann/CORBIS; 29 (LO), Underwood & Underwood/CORBIS; 30, Ctsy Guernsey's; 32, Mathew Polak/CORBIS SYGMA; 33, Hulton-Deutsch Coll./ CORBIS ; 36, WHOI; 37, 39, Emory Kristof; 40, WHOI; 42-3, Perry Thorsvik; 44-5, CORBIS; 45, Underwood & Underwood/CORBIS; 46, 46-47, Bettmann/CORBIS; 48-9, 50, Emory Kristof; 51, Titanic Hist. Soc.; 52 (UP), Ralph White/CORBIS, 52 (LO), IFE & IAO/URI-GSO; 54, 55, Bettmann/CORBIS; 56-7, 58, WHOI; 60, Titanic Hist. Soc.; 62, Ralph White/CORBIS; 63, Richard Schlecht; 64-5, Pierre Mion; 66, WHOI; 67, Ralph White/CORBIS; 69, JamesPeltekian/CORBIS SYGMA; 70, 71, 72, Ralph White/CORBIS; 75, IFE & IAO/URI-GSO; 76, Ralph White/CORBIS; 78, Matt Stone/Boston Herald/CORBIS SYGMA; 79, Ralph White/CORBIS; 81, Emory Kristof; 82-3, Ralph White/CORBIS; 83, IFE & IAO/URI-GSO; 84, Topical Press Agency/Getty Images; 84-5, IFE & IAO/URI-GSO; 86-7, Ralph White/CORBIS; 88, Dann Blackwood / WHOI; 89, Titanic Hist Soc.; 91, Davis Meltzer; 92, Al Giddings; 93, 97, David Knudsen; 98 (UP), HIP/Scala/Art Resource, NY; 98 (LO), From Dr. William Beebe; 100 (LO) and (CTR), Emory Kristof; 100 (UP), IFE & IAO/URI-GSO; 101 (UP), David McLain; 101 (LO), Ctsy NOAA; 103, Thomas J. Abercrombie; 104-5, Randy Olson; 106-7, David McLain; 108-9, IFE & IAO/URI-GSO; 109, Titanic Hist. Soc.; 110, IFE & IAO/URI-GSO; 110-1, Time Life Pictures/Getty Images; 112-3, IFE & IAO/URI-GSO; 114, Bert Fox, NGS; 115, Titanic Hist. Soc.; 117, 118-9, 120, Bert Fox, NGS; 121, Topical Press Agency/Getty Images; 122, Bert Fox, NGS; 126-7, 128, Bert Fox, NGS; 130, Ctsy Guernsey's; 133-141 (all), IFE & IAO/URI-GSO; 142, Bert Fox, NGS; 144-152 (all), IFE & IAO/URI-GSO; 153, Titanic Hist. Soc.; 155-160 (all), IFE & IAO/URI-GSO; 163, Bert Fox, NGS; 165-174 (all), IFE & IAO/URI-GSO; 175, Underwood & Underwood/CORBIS; 176-7, IFE & IAO/URI-GSO; 178, John Pratt/Keystone Features/Getty Images; 180-183 (all), IFE & IAO/URI-GSO; 184-5, WHOI; 186-7, Mosaic created by Hanumant Singh, WHOI/ ©2004 IFE. The images that make up this mosaic were taken by the HERCULES ROV during an expedition led by Dr. Robert D. Ballard from the University of Rhode Island's Institute for Archaeological Oceanography.

ADDITIONAL READING

Robert D. Ballard with Malcolm McConnell, *Adventures in Ocean Exploration:* (National Geographic, 2001); Robert D. Ballard with Rick Archbold, *The Discovery of the Titanic* (Warner Books, 1987); Robert D. Ballard with Will Hively, *The Eternal Darkness* (Princeton University Press, 2000); William J. Broad, *The Universe Below* (Simon & Schuster, 1997); Daniel Allen Butler, *"Unsinkable"* (Stackpole Books, 1998); Walter Lord, *The Night Lives On* (Morrow); Walter Lord, *A Night to Remember* (Holt, Rinehart, & Winston, 1976); Don Lynch and Ken Marschall, *Ghosts of the Abyss:* (Madison Press, 2003); Don Lynch, *Titanic* (Hyperion, 1992).

ACKNOWLEDGMENTS

ROBERT D. BALLARD: I want to thank the National Oceanic and Atmospheric Administration's (NOAA) Office of Ocean Exploration and its Director Captain Craig McLean as well as the officers and crew of NOAA's flagship the R/V BROWN. Without them, the expedition would have never happened. Next, I want to thank my team led Jim Newman and drawn from my various organizations including the Institute for Exploration in Mystic, Connecticut; the Institute for Archaeological Oceanography in the Graduate School of Oceanography at the University of Rhode Island, and the JASON Foundation for Education which provided the team needed to operate our advanced undersea technology. Special thanks to the EDS Corporation team both aboard ship and in Plano, Texas, for making our "live"exploration of the TITANIC seen by the world., to Peter Schnall and his team from Partisan Pictures for their wonderful production skills, and Jay Schadler who spent long hours on a rolling wet deck telling our story to the public at large. To Edward and Karen Kamuda of the TITANIC Historical Society for having made a replacement memorial plaque . To Dynacon and Telex for their continuing support of our expeditions. To John Ford and John Bowman at National Geographic Channel for their faith in our ability to come "live" from the deck of the TITANIC. And finally,to Terry Garcia and the Exploration Council at the National Geographic Society for letting me be an Explorer.

MICHAEL S. SWEENEY wishes to thank Earl D. Scott for his invaluable research assistance and insightful comments about the manuscript. Thanks also to Carolyn and David Sweeney, Utah State University, the skilled crew of the NOAA ship *Ronald H. Brown*, and Dr. Robert D. Ballard and his assistants. Finally, warm thanks to everyone at National Geographic, particularly Bert Fox and Barbara Brownell Grogan.

THE BOOK DIVISION thanks Bert Fox, Dr.Arthur J. Mariano and Edward H. Ryan, University of Miami, Rosenstiel School of Marine and Atmospheric Science; Dr. David M. Fratantoni, Philip L. Richardson, and Christine M. Wooding, Woods Hole Oceanographic Institution Department of Physical Oceanography;LTjg Jeremy Weirich,NOAA Office of Ocean Exploration; Kenneth S. Casey, Ph.D, NOAA National Oceanographic Data Center; Patrick Caldwell, NOAA Data Center, Hawaii; Dwight Coleman, Institute for Exploration; Dave Gittins, "All at Sea with Dave Gittins."

RETURN TO TITANIC

BY ROBERT D. BALLARD
WITH MICHAEL S. SWEENEY

PUBLISHED BY THE NATIONAL GEOGRAPHIC SOCIETY

John M. Fahey, Jr., *President and Chief Executive Officer*

Gilbert M. Grosvenor, *Chairman of the Board*

Nina D. Hoffman, *Executive Vice President*

PREPARED BY THE BOOK DIVISION

Kevin Mulroy, *Vice President and Editor-in-Chief*

Charles Kogod, *Illustrations Director*

Marianne R. Koszorus, *Design Director*

Barbara Brownell Grogan, *Executive Editor*

STAFF FOR THIS BOOK

Barbara Brownell Grogan, *Editor*

Melissa Farris, *Art Director*

Charles Kogod, *Illustrations Editor*

Susan Straight, *Illustrations and Text Researcher*

Susan Tyler Hitchcock, *Text Editor*

Carl Mehler, *Director of Maps*

Matt Chwastyk, Sven M. Dolling, Nicholas P. Rosenbach, Greg Ugiansky, *Map Research and Production*

Mike Horenstein, *Production Project Manager*

Meredith Wilcox, *Illustrations Assistant*

Margo Browning, *Release Editor*

Dianne Hosmer, *Indexer*

MANUFACTURING AND QUALITY CONTROL

Christopher A. Liedel, *Chief Financial Officer*

Phillip L. Schlosser, *Managing Director*

John T. Dunn, *Technical Director*

Maryclare McGinty, *Manager*

One of the world's largest nonprofit scientific and educational organizations, the National Geographic Society was founded in 1888 "for the increase and diffusion of geographic knowledge." Fulfilling this mission, the Society educates and inspires millions every day through its magazines, books, television programs, videos, maps and atlases, research grants, the National Geographic Bee, teacher workshops, and innovative classroom materials. The Society is supported through membership dues, charitable gifts, and income from the sale of its educational products. This support is vital to National Geographic's mission to increase global understanding and promote conservation of our planet through exploration, research, and education.

For more information, please call 1-800-NGS LINE (647-5463) or write to the following address:

National Geographic Society
1145 17th Street N.W.
Washington, D.C. 20036-4688 U.S.A.

Visit the Society's Web site at www.nationalgeographic.com.

LIBRARY OF CONGRESS CATALOGING-IN-PUBLICATION DATA

Ballard, Robert D.

  Return to Titanic / Robert D. Ballard with Michael Sweeney.

    p. cm.

  Includes bibliographical references (p.   ).

  ISBN 0-7922-7288-9

  1. Titanic (Steamship) 2. Shipwrecks--North Atlantic Ocean. 3. Underwater exploration--North Atlantic Ocean. I. Sweeney, Michael II. Title.

  G530.T6B4955 2004

  910'.9163'4--dc22